ASPEN PUBLISHERS

Casenote™ *Legal Briefs*

ADMINISTRATIVE LAW

Keyed to Courses Using

Mashaw, Merrill, and Shane's

Administrative Law: The American Public Law System

Sixth Edition

Law & Business

AUSTIN   BOSTON   CHICAGO   NEW YORK   THE NETHERLANDS

This publication is designed to provide accurate and authoritative information in regard to the subject matter covered. It is sold with the understanding that the publisher is not engaged in rendering legal, accounting, or other professional services. If legal advice or other expert assistance is required, the services of a competent professional person should be sought.

— From a Declaration of Principles adopted jointly by a Committee of the American Bar Association and a Committee of Publishers and Associates

To contact Customer Care, e-mail customer.care@aspenpublishers.com, call 1-800-234-1660, fax 1-800-901-9075, or mail correspondence to:

Aspen Publishers
Attn: Order Department
P.O. Box 990
Frederick, MD 21705

Printed in the United States of America.

1 2 3 4 5 6 7 8 9 0

ISBN 978-0-7355-8940-7

About Wolters Kluwer Law & Business

Wolters Kluwer Law & Business is a leading provider of research information and workflow solutions in key specialty areas. The strengths of the individual brands of Aspen Publishers, CCH, Kluwer Law International and Loislaw are aligned within Wolters Kluwer Law & Business to provide comprehensive, in-depth solutions and expert-authored content for the legal, professional and education markets.

CCH was founded in 1913 and has served more than four generations of business professionals and their clients. The CCH products in the Wolters Kluwer Law & Business group are highly regarded electronic and print resources for legal, securities, antitrust and trade regulation, government contracting, banking, pension, payroll, employment and labor, and health-care reimbursement and compliance professionals.

Aspen Publishers is a leading information provider for attorneys, business professionals and law students. Written by preeminent authorities, Aspen products offer analytical and practical information in a range of specialty practice areas from securities law and intellectual property to mergers and acquisitions and pension/benefits. Aspen's trusted legal education resources provide professors and students with high-quality, up-to-date and effective resources for successful instruction and study in all areas of the law.

Kluwer Law International supplies the global business community with comprehensive English-language international legal information. Legal practitioners, corporate counsel and business executives around the world rely on the Kluwer Law International journals, loose-leafs, books and electronic products for authoritative information in many areas of international legal practice.

Loislaw is a premier provider of digitized legal content to small law firm practitioners of various specializations. Loislaw provides attorneys with the ability to quickly and efficiently find the necessary legal information they need, when and where they need it, by facilitating access to primary law as well as state-specific law, records, forms and treatises.

Wolters Kluwer Law & Business, a unit of Wolters Kluwer, is headquartered in New York and Riverwoods, Illinois. Wolters Kluwer is a leading multinational publisher and information services company.

Format for the Casenote Legal Brief

Nature of Case: This section identifies the form of action (e.g., breach of contract, negligence, battery), the type of proceeding (e.g., demurrer, appeal from trial court's jury instructions), or the relief sought (e.g., damages, injunction, criminal sanctions).

Fact Summary: This is included to refresh your memory and can be used as a quick reminder of the facts.

Rule of Law: Summarizes the general principle of law that the case illustrates. It may be used for instant recall of the court's holding and for classroom discussion or home review.

Facts: This section contains all relevant facts of the case, including the contentions of the parties and the lower court holdings. It is written in a logical order to give the student a clear understanding of the case. The plaintiff and defendant are identified by their proper names throughout and are always labeled with a (P) or (D).

Palsgraf v. Long Island R.R. Co.

Injured bystander (P) v. Railroad company (D)

N.Y. Ct. App., 248 N.Y. 339, 162 N.E. 99 (1928).

Party ID: Quick identification of the relationship between the parties.

NATURE OF CASE: Appeal from judgment affirming verdict for plaintiff seeking damages for personal injury.

FACT SUMMARY: Helen Palsgraf (P) was injured on R.R.'s (D) train platform when R.R.'s (D) guard helped a passenger aboard a moving train, causing his package to fall on the tracks. The package contained fireworks which exploded, creating a shock that tipped a scale onto Palsgraf (P).

🏛 RULE OF LAW
The risk reasonably to be perceived defines the duty to be obeyed.

FACTS: Helen Palsgraf (P) purchased a ticket to Rockaway Beach from R.R. (D) and was waiting on the train platform. As she waited, two men ran to catch a train that was pulling out from the platform. The first man jumped aboard, but the second man, who appeared as if he might fall, was helped aboard by the guard on the train who had kept the door open so they could jump aboard. A guard on the platform also helped by pushing him onto the train. The man was carrying a package wrapped in newspaper. In the process, the man dropped his package, which fell on the tracks. The package contained fireworks and exploded. The shock of the explosion was apparently of great enough strength to tip over some scales at the other end of the platform, which fell on Palsgraf (P) and injured her. A jury awarded her damages, and R.R. (D) appealed.

ISSUE: Does the risk reasonably to be perceived define the duty to be obeyed?

HOLDING AND DECISION: (Cardozo, C.J.) Yes. The risk reasonably to be perceived defines the duty to be obeyed. If there is no foreseeable hazard to the injured party as the result of a seemingly innocent act, the act does not become a tort because it happened to be a wrong as to another. If the wrong was not willful, the plaintiff must show that the act as to her had such great and apparent possibilities of danger as to entitle her to protection. Negligence in the abstract is not enough upon which to base liability. Negligence is a relative concept, evolving out of the common law doctrine of trespass on the case. To establish liability, the defendant must owe a legal duty of reasonable care to the injured party. A cause of action in tort will lie where harm,

though unintended, could have been averted or avoided by observance of such a duty. The scope of the duty is limited by the range of danger that a reasonable person would foresee. In this case, there was nothing to suggest from the appearance of the parcel or otherwise that the parcel contained fireworks. The guard could not reasonably have had any warning of a threat to Palsgraf (P), and R.R. (D) therefore cannot be held liable. Judgment is reversed in favor of R.R. (D).

DISSENT: (Andrews, J.) The concept that there is no negligence unless R.R. (D) owes a legal duty to take care as to Palsgraf (P) herself is too narrow. Everyone owes to the world at large the duty of refraining from those acts that may unreasonably threaten the safety of others. If the guard's action was negligent as to those nearby, it was also negligent as to those outside what might be termed the "danger zone." For Palsgraf (P) to recover, R.R.'s (D) negligence must have been the proximate cause of her injury, a question of fact for the jury.

▶ ANALYSIS

The majority defined the limit of the defendant's liability in terms of the danger that a reasonable person in defendant's situation would have perceived. The dissent argued that the limitation should not be placed on liability, but rather on damages. Judge Andrews suggested that only injuries that would not have happened but for R.R.'s (D) negligence should be compensable. Both the majority and dissent recognized the policy-driven need to limit liability for negligent acts, seeking, in the words of Judge Andrews, to define a framework "that will be practical and in keeping with the general understanding of mankind." The Restatement (Second) of Torts has accepted Judge Cardozo's view.

Quicknotes

FORESEEABILITY A reasonable expectation that change is the probable result of certain acts or omissions.

NEGLIGENCE Conduct falling below the standard of care that a reasonable person would demonstrate under similar conditions.

PROXIMATE CAUSE The natural sequence of events without which an injury would not have been sustained.

Concurrence/Dissent: All concurrences and dissents are briefed whenever they are included by the casebook editor.

Analysis: This last paragraph gives you a broad understanding of where the case "fits in" with other cases in the section of the book and with the entire course. It is a hornbook-style discussion indicating whether the case is a majority or minority opinion and comparing the principal case with other cases in the casebook. It may also provide analysis from restatements, uniform codes, and law review articles. The analysis will prove to be invaluable to classroom discussion.

Issue: The issue is a concise question that brings out the essence of the opinion as it relates to the section of the casebook in which the case appears. Both substantive and procedural issues are included if relevant to the decision.

Holding and Decision: This section offers a clear and in-depth discussion of the rule of the case and the court's rationale. It is written in easy-to-understand language and answers the issue presented by applying the law to the facts of the case. When relevant, it includes a thorough discussion of the exceptions to the case as listed by the court, any major cites to the other cases on point, and the names of the judges who wrote the decisions.

Quicknotes: Conveniently defines legal terms found in the case and summarizes the nature of any statutes, codes, or rules referred to in the text.

Aspen Publishers is proud to offer *Casenote Legal Briefs*—continuing thirty years of publishing America's best-selling legal briefs.

Casenote Legal Briefs are designed to help you save time when briefing assigned cases. Organized under convenient headings, they show you how to abstract the basic facts and holdings from the text of the actual opinions handed down by the courts. Used as part of a rigorous study regimen, they can help you spend more time analyzing and critiquing points of law than on copying bits and pieces of judicial opinions into your notebook or outline.

Casenote Legal Briefs should never be used as a substitute for assigned casebook readings. They work best when read as a follow-up to reviewing the underlying opinions themselves. Students who try to avoid reading and digesting the judicial opinions in their casebooks or online sources will end up shortchanging themselves in the long run. The ability to absorb, critique, and restate the dynamic and complex elements of case law decisions is crucial to your success in law school and beyond. It cannot be developed vicariously.

Casenote Legal Briefs represents but one of the many offerings in Aspen's Study Aid Timeline, which includes:

- *Casenote Legal Briefs*
- *Emanuel Law Outlines*
- *Examples & Explanations* Series
- *Introduction to Law* Series
- Emanuel *Law in a Flash* Flashcards
- Emanuel *CrunchTime* Series

Each of these series is designed to provide you with easy-to-understand explanations of complex points of law. Each volume offers guidance on the principles of legal analysis and, consulted regularly, will hone your ability to spot relevant issues. We have titles that will help you prepare for class, prepare for your exams, and enhance your general comprehension of the law along the way.

To find out more about Aspen Study Aid publications, visit us online at *http://lawschool.aspenpublishers.com* or email us at *legaledu@wolterskluwer.com*. We'll be happy to assist you.

Get this Casenote Legal Brief as an AspenLaw Studydesk eBook today!

By returning this form to Aspen Publishers, you will receive a complimentary eBook download of this Casenote Legal Brief in the AspenLaw Studydesk digital format.* Learn more about AspenLaw Studydesk today at *www.AspenLaw.com*.

Name	Phone ( )
Address	Apt. No.
City	State	ZIP Code
Law School	Year (check one) ☐ 1st ☐ 2nd ☐ 3rd

Cut out the UPC found on the lower left corner of the back cover of this book. Staple the UPC inside this box. Only the original UPC from the book cover will be accepted. (No photocopies or store stickers are allowed.)

Attach UPC inside this box.

Email (Print legibly or you may not get access!)

Title of this book (course subject)

ISBN of this book (10- or 13-digit number on the UPC)

Used with which casebook (provide author's name)

Mail the completed form to: Aspen Publishers, Inc.
Legal Education Division
130 Turner Street, Bldg 3, 4th Floor
Waltham, MA 02453-8901

* Upon receipt of this completed form, you will be emailed a code for the digital download of this book in AspenLaw Studydesk format. The AspenLaw Studydesk application is available as a 60-day free trial at *www.AspenLaw.com*.

For a full list of print titles by Aspen Publishers, visit *lawschool.aspenpublishers.com*.
For a full list of digital eBook titles by Aspen Publishers, visit *www.AspenLaw.com*.

Make a photocopy of this form and your UPC for your records.

For detailed information on the use of the information you provide on this form, please see the PRIVACY POLICY at www.aspenpublishers.com.

A. Decide on a Format and Stick to It

Structure is essential to a good brief. It enables you to arrange systematically the related parts that are scattered throughout most cases, thus making manageable and understandable what might otherwise seem to be an endless and unfathomable sea of information. There are, of course, an unlimited number of formats that can be utilized. However, it is best to find one that suits your needs and stick to it. Consistency breeds both efficiency and the security that when called upon you will know where to look in your brief for the information you are asked to give.

Any format, as long as it presents the essential elements of a case in an organized fashion, can be used. Experience, however, has led *Casenotes* to develop and utilize the following format because of its logical flow and universal applicability.

NATURE OF CASE: This is a brief statement of the legal character and procedural status of the case (e.g., "Appeal of a burglary conviction").

There are many different alternatives open to a litigant dissatisfied with a court ruling. The key to determining which one has been used is to discover *who is asking this court for what.*

This first entry in the brief should be kept as *short as possible.* Use the court's terminology if you understand it. But since jurisdictions vary as to the titles of pleadings, the best entry is the one that addresses who wants what in this proceeding, not the one that sounds most like the court's language.

RULE OF LAW: A statement of the general principle of law that the case illustrates (e.g., "An acceptance that varies any term of the offer is considered a rejection and counteroffer").

Determining the rule of law of a case is a procedure similar to determining the issue of the case. Avoid being fooled by red herrings; there may be a few rules of law mentioned in the case excerpt, but usually only one is *the* rule with which the casebook editor is concerned. The techniques used to locate the issue, described below, may also be utilized to find the rule of law. Generally, your best guide is simply the chapter heading. It is a clue to the point the casebook editor seeks to make and should be kept in mind when reading every case in the respective section.

FACTS: A synopsis of only the essential facts of the case, i.e., those bearing upon or leading up to the issue.

The facts entry should be a short statement of the events and transactions that led one party to initiate legal proceedings against another in the first place. While some cases conveniently state the salient facts at the beginning of the decision, in other instances they will have to be culled from hiding places throughout the text, even from concurring and dissenting opinions. Some of the "facts" will often be in dispute and should be so noted. Conflicting evidence may be briefly pointed up. "Hard" facts must be included. Both must be *relevant* in order to be listed in the facts entry. It is impossible to tell what is relevant until the entire case is read, as the ultimate determination of the rights and liabilities of the parties may turn on something buried deep in the opinion.

Generally, the facts entry should not be longer than three to five *short* sentences.

It is often helpful to identify the role played by a party in a given context. For example, in a construction contract case the identification of a party as the "contractor" or "builder" alleviates the need to tell that that party was the one who was supposed to have built the house.

It is always helpful, and a good general practice, to identify the "plaintiff" and the "defendant." This may seem elementary and uncomplicated, but, especially in view of the creative editing practiced by some casebook editors, it is sometimes a difficult or even impossible task. Bear in mind that the *party presently* seeking something from this court may not be the plaintiff, and that sometimes only the cross-claim of a defendant is treated in the excerpt. Confusing or misaligning the parties can ruin your analysis and understanding of the case.

ISSUE: A statement of the general legal question answered by or illustrated in the case. For clarity, the issue is best put in the form of a question capable of a "yes" or "no" answer. In reality, the issue is simply the Rule of Law put in the form of a question (e.g., "May an offer be accepted by performance?").

The major problem presented in discerning what is *the* issue in the case is that an opinion usually purports to raise and answer several questions. However, except for rare cases, only one such question is really the issue in the case. Collateral issues not necessary to the resolution of the matter in controversy are handled by the court by language known as *"obiter dictum"* or merely *"dictum."* While dicta may be included later in the brief, they have no place under the issue heading.

To find the issue, ask *who wants what* and then go on to ask *why did that party succeed or fail in getting it.* Once this is determined, the "why" should be turned into a question.

The complexity of the issues in the cases will vary, but in all cases a single-sentence question should sum up the issue. *In a few cases,* there will be two, or even more rarely, three issues of equal importance to the resolution of the case. Each should be expressed in a single-sentence question.

Since many issues are resolved by a court in coming to a final disposition of a case, the casebook editor will reproduce the portion of the opinion containing the issue or issues most relevant to the area of law under scrutiny. A noted law professor gave this advice: "Close the book; look at the title on the cover." Chances are, if it is Property, you need not concern yourself with whether, for example, the federal government's treatment of the plaintiff's land really raises a federal question sufficient to support jurisdiction on this ground in federal court.

The same rule applies to chapter headings designating sub-areas within the subjects. They tip you off as to what the text is designed to teach. The cases are arranged in a casebook to show a progression or development of the law, so that the preceding cases may also help.

It is also most important to remember to *read the notes and questions* at the end of a case to determine what the editors wanted you to have gleaned from it.

HOLDING AND DECISION: This section should succinctly explain the rationale of the court in arriving at its decision. In capsulizing the "reasoning" of the court, it should always include an application of the general rule or rules of law to the specific facts of the case. Hidden justifications come to light in this entry; the reasons for the state of the law, the public policies, the biases and prejudices, those considerations that influence the justices' thinking and, ultimately, the outcome of the case. At the end, there should be a short indication of the disposition or procedural resolution of the case (e.g., "Decision of the trial court for Mr. Smith (P) reversed").

The foregoing format is designed to help you "digest" the reams of case material with which you will be faced in your law school career. Once mastered by practice, it will place at your fingertips the information the authors of your casebooks have sought to impart to you in case-by-case illustration and analysis.

B. Be as Economical as Possible in Briefing Cases

Once armed with a format that encourages succinctness, it is as important to be economical with regard to the time spent on the actual reading of the case as it is to be economical in the writing of the brief itself. This does not mean "skimming" a case. Rather, it means reading the case with an "eye" trained to recognize into which "section" of your brief a particular passage or line fits and having a system for quickly and precisely marking the case so that the passages fitting any one particular part of the brief can be easily identified and brought together in a concise and accurate manner when the brief is actually written.

It is of no use to simply repeat everything in the opinion of the court; record only enough information to trigger your recollection of what the court said. Nevertheless, an accurate statement of the "law of the case," i.e., the legal principle applied to the facts, is absolutely essential to class preparation and to learning the law under the case method.

To that end, it is important to develop a "shorthand" that you can use to make margin notations. These notations will tell you at a glance in which section of the brief you will be placing that particular passage or portion of the opinion.

Some students prefer to underline all the salient portions of the opinion (with a pencil or colored underliner marker), making marginal notations as they go along. Others prefer the color-coded method of underlining, utilizing different colors of markers to underline the salient portions of the case, each separate color being used to represent a different section of the brief. For example, blue underlining could be used for passages relating to the rule of law, yellow for those relating to the issue, and green for those relating to the holding and decision, etc. While it has its advocates, the color-coded method can be confusing and time-consuming (all that time spent on changing colored markers). Furthermore, it can interfere with the continuity and concentration many students deem essential to the reading of a case for maximum comprehension. In the end, however, it is a matter of personal preference and style. Just remember, whatever method you use, underlining must be used sparingly or its value is lost.

If you take the marginal notation route, an efficient and easy method is to go along underlining the key portions of the case and placing in the margin alongside them the following "markers" to indicate where a particular passage or line "belongs" in the brief you will write:

N   (NATURE OF CASE)
RL   (RULE OF LAW)
I   (ISSUE)
HL   (HOLDING AND DECISION, relates to the RULE OF LAW behind the decision)
HR (HOLDING AND DECISION, gives the RATIONALE or reasoning behind the decision)
HA (HOLDING AND DECISION, APPLIES the general principle(s) of law to the facts of the case to arrive at the decision)

Remember that a particular passage may well contain information necessary to more than one part of your brief, in which case you simply note that in the margin. If you are using the color-coded underlining method instead of margin notation, simply make asterisks or checks in the margin next to the passage in question in the colors that indicate the additional sections of the brief where it might be utilized.

The economy of utilizing "shorthand" in marking cases for briefing can be maintained in the actual brief writing process itself by utilizing "law student shorthand" within the brief. There are many commonly used words and phrases for which abbreviations can be substituted in your briefs (and in your class notes also). You can develop abbreviations that are personal to you and which will save you a lot of time. A reference list of briefing abbreviations can be found on page xii of this book.

C. Use Both the Briefing Process and the Brief as a Learning Tool

Now that you have a format and the tools for briefing cases efficiently, the most important thing is to make the time spent in briefing profitable to you and to make the most advantageous use of the briefs you create. Of course, the briefs are invaluable for classroom reference when you are called upon to explain or analyze a particular

case. However, they are also useful in reviewing for exams. A quick glance at the fact summary should bring the case to mind, and a rereading of the rule of law should enable you to go over the underlying legal concept in your mind, how it was applied in that particular case, and how it might apply in other factual settings.

As to the value to be derived from engaging in the briefing process itself, there is an immediate benefit that arises from being forced to sift through the essential facts and reasoning from the court's opinion and to succinctly express them in your own words in your brief. The process ensures that you understand the case and the point that it illustrates, and that means you will be ready to absorb further analysis and information brought forth in class. It also ensures you will have something to say when called upon in class. The briefing process helps develop a mental agility for getting to the *gist* of a case and for identifying, expounding on, and applying the legal concepts and issues found there. The briefing process is the mental process on which you must rely in taking law school examinations; it is also the mental process upon which a lawyer relies in serving his clients and in making his living.

acceptance	acp
affirmed	aff
answer	ans
assumption of risk	a/r
attorney	atty
beyond a reasonable doubt	b/r/d
bona fide purchaser	BFP
breach of contract	br/k
cause of action	c/a
common law	c/l
Constitution	Con
constitutional	con
contract	K
contributory negligence	c/n
cross	x
cross-complaint	x/c
cross-examination	x/ex
cruel and unusual punishment	c/u/p
defendant	D
dismissed	dis
double jeopardy	d/j
due process	d/p
equal protection	e/p
equity	eq
evidence	ev
exclude	exc
exclusionary rule	exc/r
felony	f/n
freedom of speech	f/s
good faith	g/f
habeas corpus	h/c
hearsay	hr
husband	H
in loco parentis	ILP
injunction	inj
inter vivos	I/v
joint tenancy	j/t
judgment	judgt
jurisdiction	jur
last clear chance	LCC
long-arm statute	LAS
majority view	maj
meeting of minds	MOM
minority view	min
Miranda warnings	Mir/w
Miranda rule	Mir/r
negligence	neg
notice	ntc
nuisance	nus
obligation	ob
obscene	obs
offer	O
offeree	OE
offeror	OR
ordinance	ord
pain and suffering	p/s
parol evidence	p/e
plaintiff	P
prima facie	p/f
probable cause	p/c
proximate cause	px/c
real property	r/p
reasonable doubt	r/d
reasonable man	r/m
rebuttable presumption	rb/p
remanded	rem
res ipsa loquitur	RIL
respondeat superior	r/s
Restatement	RS
reversed	rev
Rule Against Perpetuities	RAP
search and seizure	s/s
search warrant	s/w
self-defense	s/d
specific performance	s/p
statute of limitations	S/L
statute of frauds	S/F
statute	S
summary judgment	s/j
tenancy in common	t/c
tenancy at will	t/w
tenant	t
third party	TP
third party beneficiary	TPB
transferred intent	TI
unconscionable	uncon
unconstitutional	unconst
undue influence	u/e
Uniform Commercial Code	UCC
unilateral	uni
vendee	VE
vendor	VR
versus	v
void for vagueness	VFV
weight of the evidence	w/e
weight of authority	w/a
wife	W
with	w/
within	w/i
without prejudice	w/o/p
without	w/o
wrongful death	wr/d

Table of Cases

Note: There are no principal cases in Chapter 1 of the casebook.

CHAPTER **2**

The Legislative Connection

Quick Reference Rules of Law

Amalgamated Meat Cutters v. Connally

Union (P) v. Unidentified party (D)

337 F. Sup. 737 (D.D.C. 1971).

NATURE OF CASE: Constitutional challenge to the Economic Stabilization Act of 1970.

FACT SUMMARY: Amalgamated Meat Cutters (P) mounted a constitutional challenge to the Economic Stabilization Act of 1970.

🏛 RULE OF LAW
Congress may delegate to the President the power to stabilize wages and prices.

FACTS: Congress passed the 1970 Economic Stabilization Act, which empowered the President to issue executive orders stabilizing prices and wages. The Act was one of limited duration, and it mandated that any such order was to be of broad scope and not single out certain industries. It also mandated that the Executive was to develop equitable standards in implementing such an order. The President, on August 15, 1971, issued such an order. Amalgamated Meat Cutters (P), which by a contract was entitled to a wage increase shortly thereafter, challenged the Act's constitutionality.

ISSUE: May Congress delegate to the President the power to stabilize wages and prices?

HOLDING AND DECISION: (Leventhal, J.) Yes. Congress may delegate to the President the power to stabilize wages and prices. It is true that Congress may not delegate absolute legislative authority, so the question became to what extent did Congress retain control in passing the Act? The Act was of limited duration, and it mandated that any order enacted under it had to be fair, generally applicable, and have equitable standards developed. Because such standards had to be developed, access to judicial review was also preserved. This coupled with a history of legislative concern with wages and prices, persuaded the court the delegation was proper.

▶ ANALYSIS

The court was not clear as to which of the factors recited in its opinion was of the most import. Indeed, one gathers from the opinion that the court simply engaged in a balancing of the Act's potential for abuse and safeguards and found the balance tilted toward safety. To what extent a similar act without one or more of the safeguards discussed by the court would have been valid is unclear.

■══■

Quicknotes

ECONOMIC STABILIZATION ACT Allowed President to issue Executive orders setting prices and wages.

SEPARATION OF POWERS DOCTRINE Each branch of government is precluded from interfering with the authority of another.

■══■

Sun Ray Drive-In Dairy, Inc. v. Oregon Liquor Control Commission

Retail store (P) v. State agency (D)

Ore. Ct. App., 16 Or. App. 63, 517 P.2d 289 (1973).

NATURE OF CASE: Appeal of denial of liquor license.

FACTS: The Oregon Liquor Control Commission (D) denied a liquor license to Sun Ray Drive-In Dairy, Inc. (P) without following any definite set of standards.

RULE OF LAW
An administrative agency must adopt and follow specific standards upon which to base decisions.

FACTS: The Oregon Liquor Control Commission (Commission) (D) denied a liquor license to Sun Ray Drive-In Dairy, Inc. (Sun Ray) (P). The Commission (D) did not have a specific set of standards for the issuance or denial of such a license. Some factors discussed by various Commission (D) officials included store size, complaints by neighbors, and the number of local liquor outlets. However, not all Commission (D) officials used the same criteria. Sun Ray (P) appealed the license denial.

ISSUE: Must an administrative agency adopt and follow specific standards upon which to base decisions?

HOLDING AND DECISION: (Tanzer, J.) Yes. An administrative agency must adopt and follow specific standards upon which to base decisions. In the absence of such standards, neither the agency in question nor the public can possibly know how to conform their behavior in the context of the area in which that agency is involved. Also, a danger exists improper, discriminatory, or other ad hominem bases for action will be used. The rule of law is not possible without specific guidelines. Finally, judicial review is impossible without specific standards. Since the Commission (D) did not have such standards, its action was improper.

ANALYSIS

The enabling legislation in this instance gave broad discretion to the Commission (D). What factors were to be used by the Commission (D) were not spelled out by statute. As the court made clear, however, a difference exists between broad authority and unbridled authority.

■■■■

Quicknotes

JUDICIAL REVIEW The authority of the courts to review decisions, actions, or omissions committed by another agency or branch of government.

■■■■

Whitman v. American Trucking Associations, Inc.

Government agency (D) v. Trucking associations (P)

531 U.S. 457 (2001).

NATURE OF CASE: Appeal from a finding upholding a delegation of legislative power to the Environmental Protection Agency.

FACT SUMMARY: The American Trucking Associations (P) brought suit against the Environmental Protection Agency (EPA) (D), arguing that § 109(b)(1) of the Clean Air Act unconstitutionally delegated legislative power to the EPA (D) and, further, that the EPA (D) should consider implementation costs in setting air quality control standards.

 RULE OF LAW
(1) Section 109(b)(1) of the Clean Air Act constitutionally delegates legislative power to the Environmental Protection Agency.
(2) The Environmental Protection Agency may not consider the costs of implementation in setting national ambient air quality standards under § 109(b)(1) of the Clean Air Act.

FACTS: Acting under § 109(b)(1) of the Clean Air Act, the administrator of the Environmental Protection Agency (EPA) (D) revised the national air quality control standards for particulate matter and ozone. The American Trucking Associations (P) challenged the new standards. Although the federal court of appeals agreed with the Associations (P) that the delegation of legislative power to the EPA (D) was overly broad, the court held that the EPA would avoid the unconstitutional delegation by adopting a restrictive construction of § 109(b)(1). The court of appeals rejected the Associations' (P) argument that the EPA (D) should consider the cost of implementing the air quality standards in setting the air quality standards. The Associations (P) appealed.

ISSUE:
(1) Does § 109(b)(1) of the Clean Air Act constitutionally delegate legislative power to the Environmental Protection Agency?
(2) May the Environmental Protection Agency consider the costs of implementation in setting national ambient air quality standards under § 109(b)(1) of the Clean Air Act?

HOLDING AND DECISION: (Scalia, J.)
(1) Yes. Section 109(b)(1) of the Clean Air Act constitutionally delegates legislative power to the Environmental Protection Agency (EPA) (D). The text of § 109(b)(1) at a minimum requires that for a discrete set of pollutants, and based on published air quality criteria that reflect the latest scientific knowledge, the EPA (D) must establish uniform national standards at a level that is requisite to protect public health from the adverse effects of the pollutant in the ambient air. Requisite, in turn, means

sufficient, but not more than necessary. These limits on the EPA's (D) discretion closely resemble the Occupational Safety and Health Act provision, which the Supreme Court has upheld, requiring the agency to set the standard which most adequately assures, to the extent feasible, on the basis of the best available evidence, that no employee will suffer any impairment of health. Section 109(b)(1) also closely resembles agency limits in a case in which the Supreme Court permitted the Attorney General to designate a drug as a controlled substance for purposes of criminal drug enforcement if doing so was necessary to avoid an imminent hazard to the public safety. The scope of discretion § 109(b)(1) allows is in fact well within the outer limits of constitutionally permissible nondelegation precedents. Reversed as to this issue.

(2) No. As to the cost consideration issue, the EPA (D) may not consider the costs of implementation in setting national ambient air quality standards under § 109(b)(1) of the Clean Air Act. Section 109(b)(1) instructs the EPA (D) to set primary ambient air quality standards, the attainment and maintenance of which are requisite to protect the public health and within an adequate margin of safety. The text of § 109(b)(1), interpreted in its statutory and historical context, and with appreciation for its importance to the Clean Air Act as a whole, unambiguously bars cost considerations from the clean air setting process. Affirmed as to this issue.

CONCURRENCE: (Stevens, J.) It would be wiser to admit that agency rulemaking authority actually is "legislative power" hence as long as the delegation provides a sufficiently intelligible principle, there is nothing inherently unconstitutional about it.

▶ *ANALYSIS*

In the *Whitman* decision, the Supreme Court noted that the Court has never suggested that an administrative agency can cure an unlawful delegation of legislative power by adopting in its discretion a limiting construction of the statute.

■═■

Quicknotes

CLEAN AIR ACT Required certain states to establish a permit program for stationary sources of air pollution.

■═■

Immigration and Naturalization Service v. Chadha

Government agency (D) v. Immigrant (P)

462 U.S. 919 (1983).

NATURE OF CASE: Appeal of a challenge to a statute giving Congress "veto" power over executive actions.

FACT SUMMARY: The House of Representatives "vetoed" an Attorney-General decision not to deport Chadha (P).

🏛 RULE OF LAW
Congress may not reserve by statute the power to override executive enforcement of the law.

FACTS: Chadha (P), an Indian citizen, overstayed his visa, and deportation proceedings were initiated. Chadha (P) applied, pursuant to the Immigration and Naturalization Act, for a stay of deportation. The Attorney General granted the application. The House of Representatives, acting pursuant to a provision in the Act granting either house the power to override the Attorney General's decision, ordered Chadha's (P) deportation. Chadha (P) challenged the constitutionality of the House's action. The court of appeals held the House action unconstitutional.

ISSUE: May Congress reserve by statute the power to override executive enforcement of the law?

HOLDING AND DECISION: (Burger, C.J.) No. Congress may not by statute reserve the power to override executive enforcement of the law. The Constitution mandates that legislative action shall be done by approval of bills or acts by both Houses and the President or two-thirds approval by both Houses. The exceptions thereto are narrowly proscribed. Attempts at lawmaking which deviate from this framework are invalid. In overriding the execution of the law by an administrative agency, Congress engages in lawmaking. For this reason, the so-called legislative veto is unconstitutional. Affirmed.

CONCURRENCE: (Powell, J.) The Court's holding should be on narrower ground, namely, that the House in this instance improperly assumed a judicial function.

DISSENT: (White, J.) The legislative veto is an important legislative tool. Without it, Congress must either write impossible specificity into laws or refrain from delegating authority if it wishes to insist on some accountability from executive agencies. Further, the legislative veto is not lawmaking.

▶ ANALYSIS

Prior to *Chadha*, the legislative veto was becoming a more and more frequently used device. As the name implies, it was a reservation in a law of congressional power to invalidate executive enforcement. In the long battle for power that has been waged between the Executive Branch and Congress, *Chadha* was a major victory for the Executive.

■=■

Quicknotes

IMMIGRATION AND NATURALIZATION ACT Section 244 allows the Attorney General to suspend deportations for reasons of extreme hardship.

LEGISLATIVE VETO A resolution passed by one or both legislature houses that is intended to block an administrative regulation or action.

■=■

United States Department of Agriculture v. Murry

Government agency (D) v. Benefits recipient (P)

413 U.S. 508 (1973).

NATURE OF CASE: Appeal of invalidation of denial of food stamps.

FACT SUMMARY: Murry (P) was denied food stamp benefits because her ex-husband claimed certain members of her household as dependents.

🏛 RULE OF LAW

Food stamp benefits may not be denied on the basis of a conclusive presumption that households with members older than 18 years who are claimed as someone's dependent are not needy.

FACTS: The Dept. of Agriculture (D) adopted a conclusive presumption that any household wherein a member over 18 years of age was claimed as a dependent was not entitled to food stamps. This was based on the assumption that a majority of such households included college students and that such households were not needy. Murry's (P) household consisted of two sons and 10 grandchildren. Murry's (P) sole income was $57.50 in child support from her ex-husband. Murry (P) was denied food stamps because her ex-husband claimed the two sons as dependents, and they were over 18. Murry (P) challenged the denial of benefits. The court of appeals held that the denial violated due process.

ISSUE: May food stamp benefits, be denied on the basis of a conclusive presumption that households with members older than 18 years who are claimed as someone's dependent are not needy?

HOLDING AND DECISION: (Douglas, J.) No. Food stamp benefits may not be denied on the basis of a conclusive presumption that households with members older than 18 years who are claimed as someone's dependent are not needy. While the administrative convenience of conclusive presumptions is a legitimate interest, it cannot be used to override the rights of citizens to due process. Part of due process is that such presumptions be rational. The rationality of the present framework is highly suspect, as the Court does not see a relation between a deduction for the benefit of a parent of one household one year and the needs of a parent of a different household in another. Since the presumption is irrational, it violates due process. Affirmed.

CONCURRENCE: (Marshall, J.) Due process requires that hearings be granted in situations where important rights are in issue.

DISSENT: (Rehnquist, J.) It is valid for an agency to enact prophylactic limitations on the dispensation of funds, which is designed to cure systematic abuses.

▶ ANALYSIS

For a period of time in the 1970s, the Court focused a certain amount of attention on irrebuttable presumptions. However, by the 1980s it seemed that the Court, without explanation, no longer was inclined to invalidate such enactments. One wonders whether the Court quietly realized that the law is so full of such presumptions that wholesale change was neither possible nor desirable.

◼══◼

Quicknotes

DUE PROCESS The constitutional mandate requiring the courts to protect and enforce individuals' rights and liberties consistent with prevailing principals of fairness and justice and prohibiting the federal and state governments from such activities that deprive its citizens of a life, liberty, or property interest.

◼══◼

Public Citizen v. Young

Citizens' group (P) v. Food and Drug Administration (D)

831 F.2d 1108 (1987).

NATURE OF CASE: Action to reverse a Food and Drug Administration (FDA) decision.

FACT SUMMARY: Public Citizen (P) challenged the FDA's decision to list carcinogenic dyes based on risk assessments indicating that their cancer risks were trivial.

🏛 RULE OF LAW
The Delaney Clause does not contain an implicit de minimis exception for carcinogenic dyes posing trivial risks to humans.

FACTS: The Delaney Clause prohibits the Food and Drug Administration (FDA) listing of a color additive where it is found to have induced cancer in animals. In lieu of this Clause, the FDA, represented by Young (D), listed two carcinogenic dyes, Orange No. 17 and Red No. 19, for use in externally applied cosmetics. However, Public Citizen (P) challenged this dye-listing decision, even though it was based on quantitative risk assessments indicating that the cancer risks presented by the two dyes were trivial.

ISSUE: Does the Delaney Clause contain an implicit de minimis exception for carcinogenic dyes posing trivial risks to humans?

HOLDING AND DECISION: (Williams, J.) No. The Delaney Clause does not contain an implicit de minimis exception for carcinogenic dyes posing trivial risks to humans. The Clause's plain language tends to confirm a rigid prohibition against such dyes. Moreover, House committee discussions during the Clause's adoption powerfully point against any de minimis exception. Additionally, even though the food additive portion of the Clause contains an exception for substances "generally recognized" as safe, the color additive portion does not parallel it. In the instant case, if the FDA desires broader discretion in respect to listing the relevant carcinogenic dyes, then it must find relief through Congress.

▌ *ANALYSIS*

Professor Sunstein criticizes the court's result by noting primarily that the Delaney Clause "was enacted at a time when carcinogenic substances were difficult to detect and all detectable carcinogens were extremely dangerous." This, of course, no longer holds true. However, under current conditions, Professor Sunstein further notes, the "Delaney Clause almost undoubtedly increases health risks by keeping relatively safe substances off the market and by forcing consumers to resort either to noncarcinogenic substances that pose other risks or to substances that were approved by earlier administrators using the cruder technology of their day."

■═■

Quicknotes

DELANEY CLAUSE Prohibits the FDA from listing a color additive if it is a carcinogen to animals.

DE MINIMIS Frivolous or insignificant.

■═■

CHAPTER 3

Executive Supervision of Administrative Action

Quick Reference Rules of Law

Buckley v. Valeo

Member of Federal Election Commission (P) v. Opposing member (D)

424 U.S. 1 (1976).

NATURE OF CASE: Appeal of challenge to portions of the Federal Election Campaign Act of 1971.

FACT SUMMARY: Members of the Federal Election Commission were to be appointed by a method deviating from Article II, § 2 of the Constitution.

RULE OF LAW
Officers of the United States must be appointed in a manner consistent with Article II, § 2 of the Constitution.

FACTS: The Federal Election Campaign Act of 1971 created the Federal Election Campaign Commission, which was given broad sanctioning and investigative power with respect to elections. The Commission consisted of six voting members appointed by the President *pro tempore* of the Senate, the Speaker of the House, and the President, each selecting two. The Secretary of the Senate and the Clerk of the House were nonvoting members. The Act was challenged on constitutional grounds. The court of appeals upheld the section dealing with the Commission.

ISSUE: Must officers of the United States be appointed in a manner consistent with Article II, § 2 of the Constitution?

HOLDING AND DECISION: (Per curiam) Yes. Officers of the United States must be appointed in a manner consistent with Article II, § 2 of the Constitution. The Constitution provides that no member of Congress will be appointed an officer of the United States during his term. This demonstrates that the Framers intended that strict separation be maintained between executive officers and legislative officials. Further, the Constitution mandates that all such executive officials shall be nominated by the President and confirmed by the Senate. The Commission in question exercises important executive functions, and, therefore, its members are officers of the United States. This being the case, they must be appointed per the constitutional requirements of Article II. Reversed.

⯈ ANALYSIS

In theory, the Court created a fairly simple standard to follow in this area. Congress may appoint officials who perform purely legislative acts but not officers who perform executive or judicial acts. Of course, the principle is much easier in theory than in practice, and uncertainty will always exist as to which sort of officials do not have to be appointed pursuant to Article II.

Quicknotes

U.S. CONSTITUTION, ARTICLE II, § 2 Provides that the President shall nominate, with Senate's advice and consent, executive officials.

FEDERAL ELECTION CAMPAIGN ACT Created a commission to investigate and administrate Federal elections.

Bowsher v. Synar

Parties not identified.

478 U.S. 714 (1986).

NATURE OF CASE: Review of order invalidating portions of the 1985 Balanced Budget Act.

FACT SUMMARY: The 1985 Balanced Budget Act was challenged as violating the separation of powers doctrine.

🏛 RULE OF LAW
The separation of powers doctrine prevents Congress from delegating to an office subservient to it power to enforce laws.

FACTS: In 1985, Congress enacted the Balanced Budget Emergency Deficit Control Act. This law prescribed certain limits on the federal budget deficit for the years 1986 through 1991. In the event that these limits could not be met, the Act provided that the Comptroller General, the head of the General Accounting Office who is removable by joint resolution of Congress, would order certain across-the-board cuts in various federal programs. The constitutionality of the Act was challenged by a variety of plaintiffs. The district court found portions of the Act unconstitutionally violative of separation of powers, and the court of appeals affirmed.

ISSUE: Does the separation of powers doctrine prevent Congress from delegating to an office subservient to it power to enforce laws?

HOLDING AND DECISION: (Burger, C.J.) Yes. The separation of powers doctrine prevents Congress from delegating to an office subservient to it power to enforce laws. The Constitution mandates that enforcement of laws shall rest solely with the Executive. Congress may not enforce the laws. From this it follows that Congress may not delegate enforcement power to an office subservient to it. The Comptroller General, while not directly under Congress's power, may be removed by joint resolution. The power to remove is the power to control. Congress has thus left enforcement of the law in question to an office subservient to it, and this it may not do. Affirmed.

CONCURRENCE: (Stevens, J.) The Act in question essentially gives the Comptroller General the power to formulate national policy, and this vital function may not be delegated.

DISSENT: (White, J.) Vesting executive powers in non-executive officers is not a novel concept and has been approved before. The Constitution recognizes that in practice the theoretical distinctions will sometimes be violated. Only when one side seriously encroaches upon another, will the action be invalid. Such was not the case here.

DISSENT: (Blackmun, J.) The Court should strike down the provisions of the 1921 law creating the Comptroller General office which allow removal by other than impeachment.

▶ ANALYSIS

This decision came on the heels of another important separation of powers case, *INS v. Chadha*, 462 U.S. 919 (1983). This case dealt with the "legislative veto," a vehicle whereby Congress could attempt to second-guess executive action. The dissent here felt that the present law was substantially less intrusive of executive prerogatives than was the legislative veto.

Humphrey's Executor v. United States

Former FTC employee (P) v. Federal government (D)

295 U.S. 602 (1935).

NATURE OF CASE: Action to recover back pay.

FACT SUMMARY: President Roosevelt fired Humphrey, a member of the Federal Trade Commission, prior to his term's expiration, and Humphrey's executor (P) sought to recover back pay due Humphrey, now deceased.

🏛 RULE OF LAW
In the absence of congressional approval, the President may not fire administrative officials with fixed terms unless the office is purely an executive one.

FACTS: The Federal Trade Commission (FTC) was instituted by Congress to consist of five members to be appointed by the President and confirmed by the Senate for terms of seven years, removable by the President only for negligence or misfeasance. No more than three FTC members could be of the same political party. Humphrey was appointed by President Hoover in 1931. In 1934, President Roosevelt, desiring to place individuals on the FTC with his own philosophies, fired Humphrey. Following Humphrey's death in 1935, his executor (P) brought an action in the Court of Claims to recover Humphrey's salary for the period for which Humphrey would have been on the FTC but for the firing. The Court of Claims certified to the Supreme Court the issue of whether Roosevelt had the power to fire Humphrey.

ISSUE: In the absence of congressional approval, may the President fire administrative officials with fixed terms if the office is not purely an executive one?

HOLDING AND DECISION: (Sutherland, J.) No. In the absence of congressional approval, the President may not fire administrative officials with fixed terms unless the office is purely an executive one. In a purely executive office, the officer is a subordinate of the President, and his removal at will is therefore proper. However, in an administrative agency supposedly exercising independent quasi-legislative and quasi-judicial authority, it is obvious that the danger of removal at the President's will, would nullify the agency's independence. In this instance, both the terms of the Act in question and the legislative history demonstrate that Congress intended the FTC to be nonpartisan and independent, and therefore its members must be protected from removal without good cause.

▶ *ANALYSIS*

The Court struck a clear dichotomy in this case. It distinguished an earlier case wherein the Court validated the removal of a Postmaster. The Court deemed the Postmaster General's office purely an executive one, exercising no independent judgment. Where no such judgment is involved, said the Court, removal at will is permissible.

■═■

Quicknotes

FEDERAL TRADE COMMISSION ACT § 1 Allows the President to remove commissioner for cause.

■═■

Morrison v. Olson

Special prosecutor (D) v. Government official (P)

487 U.S. 654 (1988).

NATURE OF CASE: Appeal from order quashing subpoenas issued at behest of a special prosecutor.

FACT SUMMARY: The independent counsel provisions of the Ethics in Government Act were challenged as unconstitutional.

RULE OF LAW
The independent counsel provisions of the Ethics in Government Act are not unconstitutional.

FACTS: In passing the Ethics in Government Act (the Act), Congress created the office of Special Prosecutor to investigate misdeeds by government officials. The Act provided that the Attorney General must investigate allegations and report to a special judicial division, which was enabled to appoint an independent counsel which in turn would have full prosecutorial authority. The counsel could be removed only by impeachment or by the Attorney General for good cause. The Act also provided for congressional oversight. Olson (P), under investigation by Prosecutor Morrison (D), filed an action seeking to quash certain grand jury subpoenas issued at the behest of Morrison (D). The district court denied such relief, but the court of appeals reversed, holding the independent counsel portions of the Act unconstitutional. The Supreme Court accepted review.

ISSUE: Are the independent counsel provisions of the Ethics in Government Act unconstitutional?

HOLDING AND DECISION: (Rehnquist, C.J.) No. The independent counsel provisions of the Ethics in Government Act are not unconstitutional. Due to the limited scope of the counsel's office, the counsel is an inferior officer, not a principal officer that must be appointed by the President. Also, there is no constitutional prohibition on interbranch appointments, so a judicial body appointing an executive officer does not in itself violate the Constitution. This Court is of the opinion that the supervisory powers of the special division are of a ministerial nature and do not trespass on the authority of the Executive. Apart from impeachment, it is only the Attorney General who can remove the Special Prosecutor. Finally, this Court is of the opinion that the office of the Special Prosecutor does not violate the principle of separation of powers. While the Prosecutor does report to Congress, he is much more answerable to the Attorney General, who, significantly, retains the power to remove the Prosecutor. The Court believes that this does not unduly interfere with the powers of the President in enforcing the laws. For these reasons, the Court considers the office of the Special Prosecutor to be constitutional. Reversed.

DISSENT: (Scalia, J.) The independent counsel provisions of the Act essentially remove from the President prosecutorial power and place it in the hands of Congress and the Judiciary, which is a clear violation of separation of powers. The Constitution does not place some executive power in the President; it places all such power in the President. Any law altering this balance must fail.

ANALYSIS

The Appointments Clause of Article II mandates appointment of noninferior officers in the President, with consent of the Senate. The Special Prosecutor is not so appointed. The Court looked to the breadth of the Prosecutor's office and decided that although the Prosecutor has wide-ranging powers, the ad hoc nature of the office mandated a conclusion that the office was inferior.

■═■

Quicknotes

ETHICS IN GOVERNMENT ACT Allows for the appointment of special independent counsel to investigate high-ranking government officials.

■═■

Environmental Defense Fund v. Thomas

Advocacy group (P) v. Office of Management and Budget (D)

627 F. Sup. 566 (D.D.C. 1986).

NATURE OF CASE: Action to compel compliance with statutory administrative rule-making deadlines.

FACT SUMMARY: Due to extensive proposed rule review by the Office of Management and Budget (D), the Environmental Protection Agency was unable to promulgate certain rules within a statutory deadline.

🏛 RULE OF LAW
The Office of Management and Budget may not use its oversight authority to frustrate compliance with statutory deadlines.

FACTS: Congress passed certain amendments to the Resource Conservation and Recovery Act, under which the Environmental Protection Agency (EPA) (D) was to promulgate certain rules by March 1, 1985. Per Executive Order 12291, the rules were submitted to the Office of Management and Budget (OMB) (D) for review. Having serious philosophical differences as to the form the rules should take, the OMB (D) refused to clear the regulations. Several months after the proposed rules were due the Environmental Defense Fund (P) brought an action seeking an injunction compelling promulgation of the rules.

ISSUE: May the OMB use its oversight authority to frustrate compliance with statutory deadlines?

HOLDING AND DECISION: (Flannery, J.) No. The OMB (D) may not use its oversight authority to frustrate compliance with statutory deadlines. Congress enacts legislation after much deliberation and then delegates to the appropriate agency the authority to issue regulations carrying out the aims of law. To permit the OMB (D) to frustrate this by its oversight authority given under E.O. 12291 constitutes executive overreaching into the legislative sphere and cannot be considered a valid exercise of power under Article II. [The court issued an injunction mandating release of final rules by June 1, 1986.]

▶ ANALYSIS

Presidential oversight of administrative rule-making is relatively new, at least as a frequent practice. The first President to do so was Carter. Whether Congress could statutorily bar White House oversight of an administrative procedure is an issue very much undecided.

Quicknotes

RESOURCE CONSERVATION AND RECOVERY ACT Comprehensive statute designed to regulate the management of hazardous wastes.

EXECUTIVE ORDER 12291 Provided that the Environmental Protection Agency's values were to be submitted to the Office of Management and Budget.

CHAPTER 4

Administrative Adjudication

Quick Reference Rules of Law

Commodity Futures Trading Commission v. Schor

Government agency (D) v. Investor (P)

478 U.S. 833 (1986).

NATURE OF CASE: Review of dismissal of counterclaims appended to a complaint seeking reparations filed with the Commodity Futures Trading Commission.

FACT SUMMARY: Schor (P), seeking reparations from a commodities broker before the Commodity Futures Trading Commission (CFTC) (D), contended that the CFTC (D) had no jurisdiction to entertain common law counterclaims.

🏛 RULE OF LAW
The adjudication of common law counterclaims by the Commodity Futures Trading Commission is not unconstitutional.

FACTS: Schor (P), dissatisfied with the performance of certain commodity futures investments he had made, filed an action seeking reparations with the Commodity Futures Trading Commission (CFTC) (D) against Conti (D), a commodities broker. Conti (D) counterclaimed for payment of certain fees. The CFTC (D) Administrative Law Judge ruled in Conti's (D) favor in both the complaint and the counterclaim. Schor (P) then appealed, contending that the CFTC (D) had no jurisdiction to entertain common law counterclaims. The court of appeals dismissed the counterclaim, holding that the CFTC (D) lacked jurisdiction to entertain it. Conti (D) obtained review in the Supreme Court.

ISSUE: Is the adjudication of common law counterclaims by the CFTC unconstitutional?

HOLDING AND DECISION: (O'Connor, J.) No. The adjudication of common law counterclaims by the CFTC (D) is not unconstitutional. First, the CFTC (D) itself considers such jurisdiction to be valid, and the views of an administrative agency towards matters germane to it are given no small weight. More importantly, CFTC (D) jurisdiction over counterclaims in actions before it does not violate the purposes underlying Article III. Article III is meant to ensure a free and independent judiciary. It was not meant to, nor does it, confer plenary jurisdiction over all matters in Article III courts. In deciding whether the delegation of quasi-judicial power to a non-Article III court is constitutional, the main question must be whether the delegation tends to encroach on the essential attributes of judicial power. Here, this does not appear to be the case. For one, only a particularized area of law is implicated here; the CFTC (D) has not been given broad power to adjudicate common law cases. Further, decisions of the CFTC (D) Administrative Law Judges are subject to de novo review. Finally, the level of review, "weight of the evidence," is not excessively deferential. In short, the enabling statute has not expanded the power of the legislature or executive at the expense of the judiciary and, therefore, was valid. Reversed.

DISSENT: (Brennan, J.) The functions of Article III are too central to our constitutional scheme to risk their incremental erosion for the sake of legislative convenience. The exceptions that have been made to the requirements of Article III have been narrowly drawn and should remain so.

▶ ANALYSIS

Four years prior to the present action, the Court had invalidated the statutory bankruptcy system based on the same considerations discussed here. Congress had entrusted the bankruptcy system to non-Article III judges and had given them very broad powers. The Court in this action distinguished that case, *Northern Pipeline Construction Co. v. Marathon Pipe Line Co.*, 458 U.S. 50 (1982), by noting that the jurisdiction of the CFTC here was much narrower.

■=■

Quicknotes

U.S. CONSTITUTION, ARTICLE III Guarantees an independent an impartial adjudication by federal judiciary.

■=■

Goldberg v. Kelly

Welfare agency (D) v. Welfare recipient (P)

397 U.S. 254 (1970).

NATURE OF CASE: Suit alleging a denial of constitutional rights.

FACT SUMMARY: Kelly (P) and other welfare recipients alleged that they were deprived of due process because they were afforded no hearing prior to the decision of welfare authorities (D) to terminate their benefits.

🏛 RULE OF LAW
Welfare benefits may be terminated only after a hearing at which the recipient is afforded procedural safeguards, including the opportunity to be heard on his own behalf.

FACTS: Kelly (P) and other recipients of welfare assistance (P), under either the federal Aid to Families with Dependent Children (AFDC) plan or New York State's general Home Relief program, brought suit alleging that welfare officials (D) had deprived them of due process of law by deciding to terminate their benefits without first conducting a hearing concerning their continuing eligibility for aid. Subsequent to the filing of the action, welfare officials (D) of both the city and state adopted procedures which provided for limited notice and hearings prior to termination of assistance. Both procedures were designed to afford notice of the reasons for termination of benefits. However, although both procedures permitted the submission of written statements by the recipient, neither provided for a pretermination hearing at which the recipient might appear. The district court found the procedures to be constitutionally inadequate and rendered judgment in favor of the aggrieved recipients (P). The case eventually was appealed to the Supreme Court.

ISSUE: Does the Due Process Clause require a state to afford welfare recipients an evidentiary hearing prior to terminating their benefits?

HOLDING AND DECISION: (Brennan, J.) Yes. The Due Process Clause requires that welfare benefits be terminated only after a hearing at which the recipient is afforded procedural safeguards, including the opportunity to be heard on his own behalf. Welfare benefits are a matter of statutory entitlement for those eligible to receive them, and the desperate need of recipients for such benefits clearly outweighs the government's interest in summary adjudication of ineligibility. In fact the conducting of hearings prior to termination of benefits may further governmental interests, by increasing the capacity of assistance programs to "promote the general welfare." Therefore, some type of pretermination hearing must be afforded welfare recipients threatened with discontinuance of benefits, although such a hearing need not incorporate all the formalities of a judicial trial. A hearing may be deemed sufficient if it is conducted pursuant to a notice which fairly apprises the recipient of the reasons for the proposed termination of benefits, offers the recipient an opportunity to be heard on his own behalf, to confront adverse witnesses, to present arguments and evidence, and to be represented by counsel. And, needless to say, the hearing must be conducted before an impartial decision-maker. Since the procedures adopted by the welfare officials (D) of the city and state of New York fall short of guaranteeing the incidents of procedural due process herein prescribed, the judgment in favor of the complaining recipients (P) must be affirmed.

DISSENT: (Black, J.) It is probable that many welfare recipients do not meet the eligibility requirements for receipt of benefits. If the government may not suspend aid to these individuals pending ultimate determination of their ineligibility, it will lose a lot of money which it will probably be unable to recoup. Moreover, the majority's opinion will ultimately be detrimental to eligible recipients of public assistance since it will inevitably lead to pretermination hearings of such formality and expense that welfare agencies will hesitate to award benefits to anyone for fear that it will be too costly to terminate aid which is eventually determined to be unnecessary.

DISSENT: (Burger, C.J.) Due to the lack of experience in dealing with administrative welfare programs that both agencies and courts have, the Court should wait until more is known about the problems before fashioning constitutional solutions.

▶ ANALYSIS

Goldberg v. Kelly was significant in that it established that an individual may not be deprived of property rights without a prior hearing. This proposition has been adopted and expanded by subsequent cases. The effect of *Goldberg v. Kelly* is actually to guarantee two hearings—an initial determination of eligibility prior to termination and a final resolution after benefits have been discontinued. Note that the procedures prescribed by the case are in some ways more extensive than those compelled by § 554 of the Administrative Procedure Act.

■═■

Continued on next page.

Quicknotes

DUE PROCESS The constitutional mandate requiring the courts to protect and enforce individuals' rights and liberties consistent with prevailing principals of fairness and justice and prohibiting the federal and state governments from such activities that deprive its citizens of a life, liberty, or property interest.

■■■

Mathews v. Eldridge

Social Security Administration (D) v. Disability benefits recipient (P)

424 U.S. 319 (1976).

NATURE OF CASE: Appeal concerning constitutional validity of procedures on termination of disability benefits.

FACT SUMMARY: Eldridge (P) had his disability benefits terminated and brought suit.

🏛 RULE OF LAW
The Due Process Clause does not require a hearing prior to termination of disability benefits.

FACTS: The state agency and the Social Security Administration (D) terminated Eldridge's (P) disability benefits. The relevant administrative procedure was the provision of the opportunity for a claimant to assert his claim prior to any administrative action, a right to an evidentiary hearing, and subsequent judicial review before the claim became final. Instead of requesting reconsideration, Eldridge (P) commenced an action challenging the constitutional validity of the administrative procedures. The district court held that the administrative procedures pursuant to which Eldridge's (P) benefits had been terminated abridged his right to procedural due process. The court of appeals affirmed. The dispute centered on what kind of procedure was required when benefits were initially terminated, pending review. The courts below held that due process required an evidentiary hearing prior to termination.

ISSUE: Does the Due Process Clause require a hearing prior to termination of disability benefits?

HOLDING AND DECISION: (Powell, J.) No. The Due Process Clause does not require a hearing prior to termination of disability benefits. Only in *Goldberg v. Kelly*, 397 U.S. 254 (1970), has this Court held that due process requires an evidentiary hearing prior to a temporary deprivation because in that case it was emphasized that welfare assistance is given to persons on the very margin of subsistence. Eligibility for disability benefits, on the other hand, is not based on financial need. The probable value of additional procedural safeguards is not that great because termination of disability benefits turn on the routine medical reports of physicians. In considering the public interest, experience with the constitutionalizing of government procedures suggests that the ultimate additional cost in terms of money and administrative burden would be substantial. The judgment of the court of appeals is reversed.

DISSENT: (Brennan, J.) It is overly speculative for the Court to say that a discontinuance of disability benefits may cause the recipient to suffer only a limited deprivation. Moreover, the very legislative determination to provide disability benefits, without any prerequisite determination of need in fact, presumes a need by the recipient which is not the Court's function to denigrate. Indeed, here it is indicated that because disability benefits were terminated there was a foreclosure upon the recipient's home and the family's furniture was repossessed.

▶ *ANALYSIS*

The Supreme Court took on the issue of what due process procedures apply in the case of the revocation of a driver's license according to the three factors weighed in *Mathews* above. It held that: (1) a driver's license is not as important as welfare; (2) the possibility of a mistake where there is no hearing before revocation is small; (3) a prior hearing would not be administratively efficient and thus probably contrary to the public interest. Held: no prior hearing required. *Dixon v. Love*, 431 U.S. 104 (1977).

■═■

Quicknotes

DUE PROCESS The constitutional mandate requiring the courts to protect and enforce individuals' rights and liberties consistent with prevailing principals of fairness and justice and prohibiting the federal and state governments from such activities that deprive its citizens of a life, liberty, or property interest.

■═■

Hamdi v. Rumsfeld

Alleged enemy-combatant (D) v. U.S. Secretary of Defense (P)

542 U.S.507 (2004).

NATURE OF CASE: Habeas petition from designation and detention as an enemy-combatant.

FACT SUMMARY: Hamdi (D) was charged as an enemy-combatant and detained by the U.S. military. He challenged his status and the constitutionality of holding him without formal charges or proceedings.

🏛 RULE OF LAW
A United States citizen designated and detained as an enemy-combatant has a due process right to challenge that designation before a neutral arbitrator.

FACTS: On September 11, 2001, al Qaeda terrorists attacked the United States (P) and caused the deaths of 3,000 American citizens. In response, the President, authorized by Congress, sent military troops to Afghanistan to locate and subdue the terrorists and the Taliban regime supporting them. Yaser Esam Hamdi (D) was born in the United States but had lived most of his life in Saudi Arabia. He was captured by allied troops while fighting with the Taliban and turned over to the U.S. military. The Government (P) classified Hamdi (D) as an "enemy-combatant" and determined to hold him indefinitely without formal charges or proceedings. Hamdi (D) challenged this designation as unconstitutional.

ISSUE: Does a United States citizen designated and detained as an enemy-combatant have a due process right to challenge that designation before a neutral arbitrator?

HOLDING AND DECISION: (O'Connor, J.) Yes. A United States citizen designated and detained as an enemy-combatant has a due process right to challenge that designation before a neutral arbitrator. Congress did in fact authorize the detention of persons such as Hamdi (D) because Hamdi (D) was detained pursuant to an act of Congress, namely the Authorization for the Use of Military Force. It is not undisputed that Hamdi (D) was captured in a combat zone because all that is certain is that Hamdi (D) resided in that area. Hamdi (D) has not made any concessions abdicating his rights, if any, to further hearing. A citizen has a right to be free from unlawful detention without due process of law. The governmental interest in confining enemy-combatants must be balanced against the individual liberty rights of the detainee, and while it is not necessary to provide initial due process hearings for captures, those who must be detained further are entitled to further proceedings. The detainee must have an opportunity to demonstrate that the Government's (P) factual assertions are untrue.

▶ ANALYSIS

While the Court did not directly address presidential authority to designate and detain enemy-combatants, it did temper the government's attempts to unilaterally control wartime captures as they related to U.S. citizens. Although many supported the President's actions after the terrorist attacks of 2001, many more recognized the danger in resting too much power in the executive branch even in wartime. Mistakes can be made and captured U.S. citizens should be entitled to place their case before an objective party.

Quicknotes

DUE PROCESS RIGHTS The constitutional mandate requiring the courts to protect and enforce individuals' rights and liberties consistent with prevailing principles of fairness and justice, and prohibiting the federal and state governments from such activities that deprive its citizens of a life, liberty, or property interest.

HABEAS CORPUS A proceeding in which a defendant brings a writ to compel a judicial determination of whether he is lawfully being held in custody.

Board of Regents of State Colleges v. Roth

School administrator (D) v. Professor (P)

408 U.S. 564 (1972).

NATURE OF CASE: Suit to set aside an action of a state agency.

FACT SUMMARY: Roth's (P) contract as a college professor was not renewed by the Wisconsin Board of Regents of State Colleges (D).

🏛 RULE OF LAW
The state need not hold hearings or offer reasons for its failure to rehire an employee whose initial term of employment has expired.

FACTS: Roth (P) was hired to a one-year term of employment as an assistant professor at Wisconsin State University–Oshkosh. At the conclusion of that one year, he was informed by that university's president that his contract would not be renewed. According to state law, nontenured professors such as Roth (P) could be terminated without any hearing or explanation, and it was by this summary procedure that he was dismissed. Roth (P), however, filed suit against the Board of Regents of State Colleges (D), alleging that he was entitled by the Constitution to a pretermination hearing and statement of the reasons for his dismissal. In addition, he contended that he had been terminated solely because of his exercise of his right to free speech. The district court sustained Roth's (P) contention that he was entitled to the requisites of procedural due process. The court of appeals affirmed, whereupon the Supreme Court granted certiorari.

ISSUE: Is a state employee entitled to a hearing or statement of reasons for the state's failure to rehire him after his initial term of employment has expired?

HOLDING AND DECISION: (Stewart, J.) No. A state employee may not insist that the state hold hearings or offer reasons for its failure to rehire him after his initial term of employment has expired. Due process must be accorded only when an individual is threatened with deprivation of either liberty or property. Failure to rehire an employee does not abridge his liberty, unless, of course, in so doing, his employer stigmatizes him in such fashion as will restrict his freedom to seek employment elsewhere. Similarly, a contract of employment for a specific term confers upon an employee no legitimate claim to subsequent employment sufficient to constitute a property right. Accordingly, Roth (P) has made no showing that either his property or his liberty was at stake when the Board (D) acted. Therefore, he has failed to establish a right to the guarantees of procedural due process.

DISSENT: (Douglas, J.) When a state proposes to deny a privilege to one who it alleges has engaged in unprotected speech, due process requires that the state bear the burden of proving that the speech was not protected.

DISSENT: (Marshall, J.) Whenever an application for employment is denied, an employee is discharged, or a decision not to rehire an employee is made, the state must establish some reason for denying the employment.

▶ ANALYSIS

The government may fire or refuse to hire an employee, unless, in so doing, it stigmatizes him in a way which seriously forecloses future employment opportunities or deprives him of employment to which he had shown himself entitled as a matter of right, contractual or otherwise. It is doubtful, however, whether the government may dispense with the elements of due process when its basis for firing or not hiring an employee is itself unconstitutional, i.e., when it is related to the applicant's race, sex, religion, etc. In this connection, it may be noted that the Court expressly declined to consider whether the petitioner would have merited a hearing on the contention that he had been discharged for exercising his right to free speech, an issue which the Supreme Court believed itself to be foreclosed from considering.

■■■

Quicknotes

DUE PROCESS The constitutional mandate requiring the courts to protect and enforce individuals' rights and liberties consistent with prevailing principals of fairness and justice and prohibiting the federal and state governments from such activities that deprive its citizens of a life, liberty, or property interest.

■■■

Perry v. Sindermann

Junior college (D) v. Teacher (P)

408 U.S. 593 (1972).

NATURE OF CASE: Appeal from reversal of summary judgment denying relief for violation of constitutional rights.

FACT SUMMARY: Sindermann (P) challenged the validity of the nonrenewal of his teaching contract.

🏛 RULE OF LAW
Absent sufficient cause, a state may not deny its employee continued employment where denial infringes on his constitutionally protected interests or frustrates his justifiable reliance.

FACTS: After Odessa Junior College, represented by Perry (D), failed to renew Sindermann's (P) untenured teaching contract without officially stating reasons why or without granting a hearing to ascertain the basis for its decision, Sindermann (P) brought this action in federal district court, alleging that the College's (D) decision was based on his public criticism of its policies, thereby infringing on his right to freedom of speech, and that its failure to grant him a hearing violated the Fourteenth Amendment's guarantee of due process. The district court granted Perry (D) summary judgment, but the court of appeals reversed and remanded the case for a full hearing on the contested factual issues. Perry (D) appealed.

ISSUE: Absent sufficient cause, may a state deny its employee continued employment where denial infringes on his constitutionally protected interests or frustrates his justifiable reliance?

HOLDING AND DECISION: (Stewart, J.) No. Absent sufficient cause, a state may not deny its employee continued employment where denial infringes on his constitutionally protected interests or frustrates his justifiable reliance. This Court has long recognized the impermissibility of governmental denial of a benefit when denial infringes on constitutionally protected interests, even where the benefit is the right to be reemployed. Moreover, in respect to justifiable reliance, when an employee justifiably relies upon an employer's words or acts that demonstrate an implied agreement between them, then the employer's severance of this agreement must be accompanied by a sufficient justification in order to be permissible. In the instant case, there existed a genuine issue of material fact as to the following: (1) whether the College (D) refused to renew Sindermann's (P) teaching contract as a reprisal for his exercise of constitutionally protected rights and (2) whether the College's (D) words or actions demonstrated an implied agreement between it and Sindermann (P) to maintain his employment absent sufficient cause. Accordingly, the College officials (D) were obligated to grant Sindermann (P) a hearing so that he could be informed of the grounds for his nonretention and challenge their sufficiency. Affirmed.

▶ ANALYSIS

Some criticism by government employees is protected by the First Amendment, *Pickering v. Board of Education*, 391 U.S. 563 (1968). Additionally, the Supreme Court has recognized a constitutional right not to be fired for the exercise of First Amendment rights, e.g., *Branti v. Finkel*, 445 U.S. 507 n. 3 (1980). Interestingly enough, however, the Court, upon remanding the instant case, avoided directly endorsing Sindermann's (P) assertion that his liberty interests were infringed.

■=■

Quicknotes

FOURTEENTH AMENDMENT Declares that no state shall make or enforce any law which shall abridge the privileges and immunities of citizens of the United States.

■=■

Cleveland Board of Education v. Loudermill

School administration (D) v. Former employee (P)

470 U.S. 532 (1985).

NATURE OF CASE: Appeals from denials of relief from public employment termination.

FACT SUMMARY: Loudermill (P) and Donnelly (P) contended they were entitled to hearings prior to their public employment being terminated.

🏛 RULE OF LAW
There is a property right in continued public employment which cannot be terminated without due process of law.

FACTS: Loudermill (P) and Donnelly (P), in separate cases consolidated on appeal, were terminated from public employment without a prior hearing. They sued, contending this violated due process. The governmental entities contended they had no protectable liberty or property interest entitled to due process protection. The district court dismissed the action for failure to state a claim upon which relief could be granted. The court of appeals reversed and the Supreme Court granted certiorari.

ISSUE: Is there a protectable property right in continued public employment which cannot be terminated without due process of law?

HOLDING AND DECISION: (White, J.) Yes. There is a protectable property right in continued public employment which cannot be terminated without due process of law. The state statute under which the plaintiffs were hired classifies them as public employees entitled to continued employment during good behavior and efficient service. Thus termination could come only after a finding of an absence of either of these two factors. This requires a pretermination opportunity to respond and a post-termination hearing. Thus the court of appeals decision is affirmed.

DISSENT: (Rehnquist, J.) There is no property right in continued public employment.

▌ ANALYSIS

The Court in this case followed its earlier decision in *Arnett v. Kennedy*, 416 U.S. 134 (1974). In that case employment was under a federal statute. The statute provided for 30 days' notice prior to termination, yet no evidentiary prior hearing.

■━■

Quicknotes

DUE PROCESS The constitutional mandate requiring the courts to protect and enforce individuals' rights and liberties consistent with prevailing principals of fairness and justice, and prohibiting the federal and state governments from such activities that deprive its citizens of a life, liberty, or property interest.

PRETERMINATION HEARING A hearing held prior to the termination of a property interest.

■━■

United States v. Florida East Coast Railway Co.

Government (D) v. Railroad company (P)

410 U.S. 224 (1973).

NATURE OF CASE: Appeal of nullification of certain boxcar compensation rules.

FACT SUMMARY: The Interstate Commerce Commission adopted rules regarding per diem charges on boxcars following an informal conference.

🏛 RULE OF LAW
The Interstate Commerce Commission need not hold a formal hearing prior to establishing rules with respect to car service by common carriers.

FACTS: Amendments to the Interstate Commerce Act empowered the Interstate Commerce Commission (ICC) (D) to adopt rules with respect to car service by common carriers and particularly to the compensation to be paid car owners for borrowed boxcars. The ICC (D) obtained data on freight-car demand from various carriers. In response to concerns expressed by various carriers, the ICC (D) held an informal conference. The ICC (D) subsequently published rule proposals inviting criticism. The proposals were then adopted. The ICC's (D) actions were challenged for failure to hold a formal hearing. The lower court invalidated the ICC's (D) actions.

ISSUE: Must the ICC hold a formal hearing prior to establishing rules with respect to car service by common carriers?

HOLDING AND DECISION: (Rehnquist, J.) No. The ICC need not hold a formal hearing prior to establishing rules with respect to car service by common carriers. The Administrative Procedure Act states the evidentiary requirements for formal hearings but does not mandate that formal hearings always be held. When a statute does not expressly require a formal hearing, the agency in question may, when conducting rulemaking, take evidence by written submission if the agency believes a formal hearing unnecessary. Here, the ICC (D) took extensive steps to obtain evidence through written submission. Since this Court has already held that the Interstate Commerce Act does not require hearings, the ICC's (D) actions were proper. Reversed.

DISSENT: (Douglas, J.) The Act should be interpreted to require a hearing.

▶ ANALYSIS

The Court's opinion here took a very narrow view of the necessity for formal hearings. The Interstate Commerce Act amendment in question did contain language suggesting a hearing would be necessary, but the Court found the language insufficient to trigger the requirement of a hearing. It would seem that only statutes clearly spelling out the requirement of a hearing will bring the Administrative Procedure Act's rules for formal hearings into play.

■▬■

Quicknotes

INTERSTATE COMMERCE ACT § 1 (14) Allows the Commission to prescribe per diem charges for the use of one railroad cars owned by another.

PRETERMINATION HEARING A hearing held prior to the termination of a property interest.

APA § 553 Establishes the minimum requirements of public rulemaking procedure.

■▬■

Richardson v. Perales

Department of Health, Education, and Welfare (D) v. Injured worker (P)

402 U.S. 389 (1971).

NATURE OF CASE: Appeal from award of Social Security benefits.

FACT SUMMARY: In Perales's (P) action to contest a hearing examiner's reliance on written medical evidence as a basis for denying him Social Security benefits, the court of appeals denied the validity of the written evidence in the face of live contradictory testimony in favor of Perales (P).

🏛 **RULE OF LAW**
Written medical reports may constitute "substantial evidence" within the meaning of § 205(g) of the Social Security Act, even though live testimony is contradictory.

FACTS: After an adverse judgment before a hearing examiner, Perales (P) brought this action to federal court, seeking compensation under the Social Security Act for his alleged inability to work due to back problems. In his ruling against Perales (P), the examiner relied, in important part, on written examining-physician medical reports which contradicted Perales's (P) live testimony. In reviewing this judgment, the Fifth Circuit Court of Appeals reversed, holding that the written evidence was not "substantial" within the meaning of § 205(g) of the Act when it was contradicted by evidence from the live witnesses. Richardson (D), the Secretary of Health, Education, and Welfare, appealed.

ISSUE: May written medical reports constitute "substantial evidence" within the meaning of § 205(g) of the Social Security Act, even though live testimony is contradictory?

HOLDING AND DECISION: (Blackmun, J.) Yes. Written medical reports may constitute "substantial evidence" within the meaning of § 205(g) of the Social Security Act, even though live testimony contradicts the written evidence during a hearing. Congress has granted adjudicators in this context broad discretion to establish hearing procedures. As a result of this emphasis on the informal, evidence normally inadmissible under normal court procedures may be admitted at the adjudicator's discretion if its admittance affords a claimant a reasonable opportunity for a fair hearing. In the instant case, since the physicians' reports were on file and available for inspection by Perales (P), the authors of those reports were known and available for subpoena and cross-examination purposes, and the specter of questionable credibility and veracity was not present. The administrator's decision appeared to be reasonably supported, even though Perales's (P) live testimony contradicted the reports. Reversed and remanded.

DISSENT: (Douglas, J.) Cross-examination of doctors in physical injury cases is essential to a full and fair disclosure of the facts.

▶ **ANALYSIS**

Perales follows a modern trend in apparently rejecting the so-called residuum rule. Under this rule, a court could not uphold an agency order under the test of "substantial evidence" unless the record contained at least a "residuum" of nonhearsay support for the underlying fact-finding. Many states still hold to the rule that administrative hearings can allow hearsay testimony but that any decision from such hearings cannot be based solely on hearsay evidence.

■═■

Quicknotes

SOCIAL SECURITY ACT, § 205 Sets the standards for Social Security benefits hearings.

■═■

Nash v. Califano

Administrative law judge (P) v. Social Security Administrator (D)

613 F.2d 10 (2d Cir. 1980).

NATURE OF CASE: Appeal of dismissal of challenge to certain regulations imposed on Social Security Administrative Law Judges.

FACT SUMMARY: The Social Security Administration imposed certain work product restrictions on Administrative Law Judges in the Administration.

🏛 RULE OF LAW
Social Security Administrative Law Judge has standing to attack work product restrictions on such judges.

FACTS: The Social Security Administrative Procedure Act vested in certain officers, called Administrative Law Judges (ALJs), the right to hear Social Security appeals. The judges were also given salary and tenure independence from the Administration. In 1975, the Administration's Bureau of Hearings and Appeals instituted certain regulations designed to reduce a serious case backlog. The regulations concerned how hearings would be held, mandated a proper reversal rate, and set certain speed quotas. Nash (P), an ALJ, challenged this as a violation of his statutory independence. The district court dismissed for lack of standing.

ISSUE: Does a Social Security Administrative Law Judge have standing to attack work product restrictions on such judges?

HOLDING AND DECISION: (Kaufman, C.J.) Yes. A Social Security Administrative Law Judge has standing to attack work product restrictions on such judges. Provisions of the Administrative Procedure Act clearly confer a qualified right of decisional independence upon ALJs. Since the independence is expressed in personal terms such as compensation and tenure, the conclusion must be that ALJs have a sufficiently personal interest in challenges to their independence to permit them to take their grievances to court. Reversed.

▶ ANALYSIS

The court here never says exactly what sort of right of which Nash (P) was claiming deprivation. Was independence a property right or a liberty interest? The court did not need to say because it was not reaching the merits of the claim.

Quicknotes

STANDING Whether a party possesses the right to commence suit against another party by having a personal stake in the resolution of the controversy.

ARTICLE III, U.S. CONSTITUTION Limits federal judicial power to cases and controversies.

Heckler v. Campbell

Department of Health and Human Services (D) v. Benefits claimant (P)

461 U.S. 458 (1983).

NATURE OF CASE: Appeal of administrative denial of disability benefits.

FACT SUMMARY: Campbell (P) was denied disability benefits when the Department of Health and Human Services (D), using published guidelines, determined that she was not disabled.

🏛 RULE OF LAW
The Department of Health and Human Services may rely on published medical-vocational guidelines to determine a claimant's right to Social Security disability benefits.

FACTS: The Department of Health and Human Services (D) adopted regulations which factored in a disability claimant's age, health, education, and experience and set forth rules regarding whether a significant number of jobs would exist for which the applicant was qualified. If such jobs did exist, then benefits would be denied. Prior to these rules, vocational experts made determinations on a case-by-case basis. Campbell (P) was denied benefits after use of the adopted guidelines. The Social Security Appeals Council and the district court upheld the decision, but the court of appeals reversed, holding that the Department of Health and Human Services (D) must identify specific alternative jobs for an applicant.

ISSUE: May the Department of Health and Human Services, rely on published medical-vocational guidelines to determine a claimant's right to Social Security disability benefits?

HOLDING AND DECISION: (Powell, J.) Yes. The Department of Health and Human Services may rely on published medical-vocational guidelines to determine a claimant's right to Social Security disability benefits. Contrary to Campbell's (P) assertions, the findings of the Department of Health and Human Services (D) here were individualized. The Department of Health and Human Services (D) had to compare her qualifications with the standards adopted and then make the determination. The requirement of individualized treatment does not prohibit an agency from using standards not requiring case-by-case treatment. The present method affords claimants ample opportunity to present evidence. Only after considering this evidence was the decision made. There is nothing unacceptable about this procedure. Reversed.

▶ ANALYSIS

The Court, as far as the opinion indicates, did not really address what the court of appeals seemed to think important. The court of appeals held that the Department of Health and Human Services (D) must list the specific jobs available to an applicant. The Court did not address this but merely held the Department of Health and Human Services (D) procedure valid.

■═■

Air Line Pilots Association v. Quesada

Union (P) v. Federal Aviation Administration (D)

276 F.2d 892 (2d Cir. 1960).

NATURE OF CASE: Appeal from denial of preliminary injunction against airline pilots' mandatory retirement age rule.

FACT SUMMARY: In the Air Line Pilots Association's (ALPA's) (P) action to nullify a Federal Aviation Agency regulation prohibiting commercial airline pilots from flying beyond age 60, the district court denied ALPA's (P) motion for a preliminary injunction despite ALPA's (P) claim that no hearings were held in support of the regulation.

🏛 RULE OF LAW
Under the Federal Aviation Act, the Administrator of the Federal Aviation Agency is free to promulgate reasonable rules which adequately provide for national security and safety in air commerce.

FACTS: After Quesada (D), Administrator of the Federal Aviation Agency, promulgated a regulation that established a 60-year maximum age requirement for pilots, the Air Line Pilots Association (ALPA) (P) moved for a preliminary injunction in federal district court, seeking to nullify the regulation's application since it was issued without adjudicatory hearings being held. Notwithstanding ALPA's (P) complaints, however, the district court denied the motion. ALPA (P) appealed.

ISSUE: Under the Federal Aviation Act, is the Administrator of the Federal Aviation Agency free to promulgate reasonable rules which adequately provide for national security and safety in air commerce?

HOLDING AND DECISION: (Lumbard, C.J.) Yes. Under the Federal Aviation Act, the Administrator of the Federal Aviation Agency is free to promulgate reasonable rules which adequately provide for national security and safety in air commerce. Congress has granted the administrator broad discretion under this act in lieu of his presumed expertise in serving the public interest. As a result of this presumption, the administrator is free to formulate administrative regulations which limit in the public interest the use that persons may make of their property or privileges without affording each one affected the opportunity to present evidence upon the fairness of the regulation (see *Bowles v. Willingham*, 321 U.S. 503 [1944]). Moreover, the speedy adoption of these regulations far outweighs any possible advantage in a multitude of piecemeal and time-consuming hearings brought by those affected by them. In the instant case, since the establishment of a 60-year maximum age requirement for pilots appeared reasonably related to promoting public safety, ALPA's (P) preliminary-injunctive motion was properly denied. Affirmed.

▶ ANALYSIS

Later suits seeking to keep sexagenarian pilots aloft have been no more successful than ALPA's. Various pilots sought to circumvent the rule through an exceptions process, and courts of appeals warned that a refusal to consider the impact of advances in medical technology on the reasonableness of denying exemptions might result in the invalidity of the rule. See, e.g., *Starr v. FAA*, 589 F.2d 307, 314 (7th Cir. 1978).

■=■

Quicknotes

FEDERAL AVIATION ACT, § 609 Sets standards for adjudicatory hearings under the Act.

ADJUDICATORY PROCEEDING A hearing conducted by an administrative agency resulting in a final judgment regarding the rights of the parties involved.

■=■

CHAPTER 5

Administrative Rulemaking

Quick Reference Rules of Law

National Petroleum Refiners Association v. Federal Trade Commission

Trade organization (P) v. Government agency (D)

482 F.2d 672 (D.C. Cir. 1973).

NATURE OF CASE: Appeal of challenge to Federal Trade Commission statutory rulemaking power.

FACT SUMMARY: The National Petroleum Refiners Association (P) challenged the power of the Federal Trade Commission (D) to promulgate substantive rules of business conduct.

🏛 RULE OF LAW
The Federal Trade Commission has statutory power to promulgate substantive rules of business conduct.

FACTS: The Federal Trade Commission (FTC) (D) adopted a rule that failure to post octane rating numbers on gasoline pumps at service stations was a deceptive business practice. The National Petroleum Refiners Association (P) attacked this rule on the basis that the FTC (D) had no statutory power to issue such rules and that its power was merely adjudicatory. The district court upheld this argument and held the rule invalid. The FTC (D) appealed.

ISSUE: Does the FTC have statutory power to promulgate substantive rules of business conduct?

HOLDING AND DECISION: (Wright, J.) Yes. The FTC (D) has statutory power to promulgate substantive rules of business conduct. The FTC's (D) enabling act does not limit the FTC (D) to a purely adjudicative role and, in fact, contains sections giving the FTC (D) rulemaking power. Other courts have long held that the FTC (D) has rulemaking power, and similar federal agencies are recognized to have such rulemaking power. Allowing such an agency to have such power gives it invaluable resource-saving flexibility in regulation and carries little danger of abuse since statutory standards exist. For these reasons, this court holds that the FTC (D) does possess rulemaking power. Reversed.

▶ ANALYSIS

Arguments exist on both sides of the issue as to whether or not vesting rulemaking power in an agency such as the FTC raises the specter of abuse of power. On one side, it is argued that agency rules constrain excessive discretion. On the other hand, such rulemaking is seen as a method of consolidating and increasing agency power and encroaching on the legislative branch.

Quicknotes

15 U.S.C. § 46 (SECTION 6(g)) Specifically provides for rulemaking with regard to carrying out provisions of the Act.

Pacific States Box & Basket Co. v. White

Fruit container manufacturer (P) v. State agency (D)

296 U.S. 176 (1935).

NATURE OF CASE: Appeal of challenge to rule-making authority of an administrative agency.

FACT SUMMARY: The Oregon Division of Plant Industry (D) issued an order regarding the legitimate size and shape of raspberry and strawberry containers, which effectively ended Pacific States Box & Basket Co.'s (P) Oregon market.

🏛 RULE OF LAW

An appropriate agency has authority to mandate the size and shape of fruit containers.

FACTS: Pacific States Box & Basket Co. (Pacific States) (P) sold fruit containers in Oregon. The Oregon Division of Plant Industry (D) promulgated rules regarding the permissible shape and size of such containers for strawberries and raspberries. Pacific States (P) did not have containers meeting the specifications. Pacific States (P) challenged the agency action as being in excess of its authority. The lower court upheld the regulations.

ISSUE: Does an appropriate agency have authority to mandate the size and shape of fruit containers?

HOLDING AND DECISION: (Brandeis, J.) Yes. An appropriate agency has authority to mandate the size and shape of fruit containers. Only when such regulations are arbitrary and capricious will they be struck down. Furthermore, a presumption of validity attaches to such regulations when they are adopted by an agency of duly delegated authority, and only when a challenger can demonstrate that no possible valid motive for the regulation exists will the regulation be struck down. Here, the agency involved was responsible for maintaining the integrity of Oregon's agriculture, and to promulgate rules regarding packaging was clearly an exercise of proper rulemaking authority, as packaging is obviously important to proper transport and preservation of perishables. Affirmed.

▶ ANALYSIS

By the time of this ruling, the era of substantive due process had ended, so the result is not surprising. The real core of the decision was the discussion of the presumption of validity. Statutes have always had such a presumption of validity. To so hold for regulations gives administrative regulations legitimacy close to that of statutes.

Quicknotes

ARBITRARY AND CAPRICIOUS STANDARD Standard imposed in reviewing the decision of an agency or court when the decision may have been made in disregard of the facts or law.

Automotive Parts & Accessories Association v. Boyd

Trade organization (P) v. Transportation department (D)

407 F.2d 330 (D.C. Cir. 1968).

NATURE OF CASE: Appeal of government adoption of auto safety standards.

FACT SUMMARY: The Department of Transportation (D) promulgated, via an informal procedure, certain regulations mandating factory installation of automobile head restraints.

🏛 **RULE OF LAW**
▥ Regulations promulgated under the National Traffic and Motor Vehicle Safety Act of 1966 may be adopted informally.

FACTS: The National Traffic and Motor Vehicle Safety Act of 1966 prescribed both informal and formal hearing-type procedures for adopting auto safety regulations. The Department of Transportation (D) published certain proposals for auto safety and invited public response. One proposal was for mandatory factory installation of head restraints. The proposal was adopted without a formal hearing, after public response was reviewed. The Automotive Parts & Accessories Association (P) petitioned for reconsideration. Upon reconsideration, the rule was upheld. The Automotive Parts & Accessories Association (P) appealed.

ISSUE: May regulations promulgated under the National Traffic and Motor Vehicle Safety Act of 1966, be adopted informally?

HOLDING AND DECISION: (McGowan, J.) Yes. Regulations promulgated under the National Traffic and Motor Vehicle Safety Act of 1966 (the Act) may be adopted informally. The main inquiry into the permissibility of this consists of looking at the Act itself and its legislative history. The Act prescribes the sort of informal procedure used by the Department of Transportation (D) here. Also, legislative history tends to show that Congress intended that informal rulemaking would be the norm and formal hearings the exception. Contrary to Automotive Part & Accessories Association's (P) assertions, informal rulemaking does not preclude judicial review, as records do exist (a court may review the initial rule proposal and the public response thereto). Since the Act provides for informal rulemaking and judicial review is not threatened, informal rulemaking under the Act is proper. [The court went on to hold that the rule adopted was rational.] Affirmed.

▸ **ANALYSIS**

Generally speaking, administrative actions are contemplated to be subject to judicial review. The Administrative Procedure Act so states. As the court here indicates, judicial review need not require a formal hearing and transcript in the administrative action below. The manner of review is somewhat determined by the type of procedure used by the administrative agency.

■▬■

Quicknotes

ADMINISTRATIVE PROCEDURE ACT (APA) Enacted in 1946 to govern practices and proceedings before federal administrative agencies.

NATIONAL TRAFFIC AND MOTOR VEHICLE SAFETY ACT provides that the APA shall apply to all orders establishing standards.

■▬■

National Tire Dealers & Retreaders Association, Inc. v. Brinegar

Trade organization (P) v. Transportation department (D)

491 F.2d 31 (D.C. Cir. 1974).

NATURE OF CASE: Appeal of government tire regulations.

FACT SUMMARY: The Department of Transportation (D) promulgated rules mandating the permanent impression of certain information onto retreaded tires.

🏛 RULE OF LAW
Rules promulgated under a legislative enactment must reasonably advance the purposes of the enactment.

FACTS: The Department of Transportation (D) adopted, under the National Traffic and Motor Vehicle Safety Act of 1966, regulations mandating that certain information be permanently imprinted on retreaded tires. This included information regarding size, inflation pressure, and other specifications. The Department of Transporation (D) did not make any findings that such information was likely to be needed beyond the time of initial purchase. The National Tire Dealers and Retreaders Association (P) challenged the rules, producing evidence that adopting the rules would be prohibitively expensive for the industry.

ISSUE: Must rules promulgated under a legislative enactment reasonably advance the purposes of the enactment?

HOLDING AND DECISION: (Wilkey, J.) Yes. Rules promulgated under a legislative enactment must reasonably advance the purposes of the enactment. While agencies have broad rulemaking power under most legislative enactments, a substantial relationship between the purpose and means must be demonstrated. Here, the labeling of retreaded tires is undoubtedly important when the tires are sold, but no evidence exists to show it is important thereafter. When this is weighed against substantial assertions of severe economic hardship in complying with the rules, it seems that no such substantial relationship between the rules in question and auto safety exists.

▶ ANALYSIS

While not saying so, the court here clearly adopted a balancing approach. The court found the tenuous claims of advanced safety outweighed by real economic detriments. The court itself said that the tenuous safety connection might have passed judicial scrutiny had it not been for the countervailing economic considerations.

Quicknotes

NATIONAL TRAFFIC AND MOTOR VEHICLE SAFETY ACT, § 201 Mandates that pneumatic tires be labeled.

STANDARD 117 Provides specific rules for tire labeling.

Motor Vehicle Manufacturers Association of U.S., Inc. v. State Farm Mutual Automobile Insurance Co.

Parties not identified.

463 U.S. 29 (1983).

NATURE OF CASE: Appeal from decision finding agency action arbitrary and capricious.

FACT SUMMARY: The National Highway Traffic Safety Administration (D) appealed from a decision of the court of appeals finding that the revocation of the requirement that new motor vehicles produced after September 1982 be equipped with passive restraints to protect occupants in the event of a collision was arbitrary and capricious.

🏛 RULE OF LAW
When an agency modifies or rescinds a previously promulgated rule, it is required to supply a satisfactory, rational analysis supporting its decision.

FACTS: Standard 208 is a rule promulgated by the Department of Transportation dealing with motor vehicle occupant safety. In 1969, the standard first included a requirement that cars come equipped with a passive restraint system. Between 1976 and 1980 a mandatory passive restraint requirement was issued. The two systems that would satisfy the standard would be an air bag system or a passive seat belt system, with the choice of system being left up to the manufacturer. It was assumed that manufacturers would install approximately 60% air bags and 40% passive belts. By 1981, the manufacturers planned to produce 99% of their cars equipped with passive belts. In 1981, even though studies, surveys, and other empirical evidence indicated that the use rate associated with the passive belts was more than double that associated with manual belts, the National Highway Traffic Safety Administration (NHTSA) (D) concluded that the safety benefits associated with the standard's implementation did not justify the costs of implementing the standard. The NHTSA (D), without considering the possible use of air bags, rescinded the passive restraint requirement. The court of appeals found that the NHTSA's (D) revocation of the passive restraint requirement was arbitrary and capricious, and the NHTSA (D) appealed.

ISSUE: When an agency rescinds or modifies a previously promulgated rule, is it required to supply a satisfactory, rational analysis supporting its decision?

HOLDING AND DECISION: (White, J.) Yes. When an agency rescinds or modifies a previously promulgated rule, it is required to supply a satisfactory, rational analysis supporting its decision. A change or rescission is akin to the promulgation of the rule itself and is subject to the same arbitrary and capricious standard. The agency must show a rational connection between the facts found and the decision rendered. The National Traffic and Motor Vehicle Safety Act of 1966 (Act) mandates the achievement of traffic safety. Given the conceded effectiveness of air bags, the logical response to the manufacturers' actions would have been to require air bags. Not only was this not done, it appears that the NHTSA (D) did not even consider it. A rational rescission decision cannot be made without the consideration of technologically feasible alternatives of proven value. Further, the empirical evidence runs counter to the agency's determination that the safety aspects associated with the use of passive belts could not be determined. The empirical evidence indicates that there is a doubling of use over the use of manual belts, and the safety benefits associated with the increased use of safety belts is unquestioned. Finally, the NHTSA (D) has failed to articulate a basis for not requiring nondetachable passive belts. By failing to consider feasible, logical alternatives and dismissing the safety benefits associated with passive restraints in light of the evidence, the NHTSA (D) has failed to present an adequate basis or explanation for rescinding the mandatory passive restraint requirement. Vacated and remanded.

CONCURRENCE AND DISSENT: (Rehnquist, J.) Since the airbag and seatbelt were explicitly approved in the standard the agency was rescinding, the agency should explain why it declined to leave those requirements intact. The agency's explanation, while by no means a model, is adequate. Furthermore, as long as the agency remains within the bounds established by Congress, it is entitled to assess administrative records and evaluate priorities in light of the philosophy of the administration.

▶ ANALYSIS

Standard-setting by the NHTSA (D) has proved most troublesome. Initial promulgation of standards was in large part mere adoptions of already existing standards. The promulgation of new standards is associated with a whole host of problems, including the problem of obtaining accurate information and the problem of enforcement and the problems that may be encountered in negotiating such standards with industry and other interest groups.

Quicknotes

STANDARD 208 Required that passive restraints protect auto passengers.

American Mining Congress v. Mine Safety & Health Administration

Trade group (P) v. Government agency (D)

995 F.2d 1106 (D.C. Cir. 1993).

NATURE OF CASE: Judicial review of administrative action.

FACT SUMMARY: The Mine Safety & Health Administration contended that Program Policy Letters—designed to state its position that certain issued x-ray readings should qualify as "diagnoses" of lung disease-should be exempt from rulemaking requirements.

> ## 🏛 RULE OF LAW
> An agency pronouncement will be subject to Administrative Procedure Act notice-and-comment requirements if it has legal effect.

FACTS: Under statutory authority adopted via notice-and-comment rulemaking, mine operators were required to report any diagnosis of certain occupational illnesses. An operator's failure to report such illnesses within ten days would lead to citation and penalty. Through a series of Program Policy Letters (PPLs), issued in response to inquiries from mine operators, the Mine Safety & Health Administration (MSHA) (D) stated that a chest x-ray reading above a specified level constituted a "diagnosis" of lung disease and triggered the reporting requirement. The American Mining Congress (P) brought suit claiming that the PPLs were void under the Administrative Procedure Act for failure to follow the public notice and comment requirements of § 553. In defending its omission of notice and comment, the MSHA (D) claimed the PPLs were interpretive rules and therefore did not statutorily require notice and comment.

ISSUE: Will an agency pronouncement be subject to APA notice-and-comment requirements if it has legal effect?

HOLDING AND DECISION: (Williams, J.) Yes. An agency pronouncement will be subject to APA notice-and-comment requirements if it has legal effect. To determine whether the interpretive rules in question have a legal effect, a court must examine four factors. First, in absence of the rule, is there no other means by which the agency can enforce the performance of duties or confer benefits? Second, was the rule published in the Code of Federal Regulations? Third, did the agency explicitly invoke its legislative authority as granted by Congress? Fourth, does the rule amend a prior legislative rule? If the answer to any of these questions is "yes," then the rule is legislative, not interpretive. Here, the PPLs are interpretative rules. Statutory regulations already required mine operators to report occupational illnesses. Further, the PPLs were not published in the Code of Federal Regulations, nor did MSHA (D) invoke its general legislative authority. Finally, the PPLs do not function as amendments merely because they supply more detailed interpretations of statutory guidelines. Affirmed.

▶ ANALYSIS

These rules and statements merely function to clarify. They provide guidance to the public as well as to agency staff and decision makers.

■▬■

Quicknotes

APA, § 553 Provides for exemptions from notice and comment rulemaking.

NOTICE AND COMMENT Informal rulemaking.

■▬■

United States v. Nova Scotia Food Products Corp.

Federal government (P) v. Food company (D)

568 F.2d 240 (2d Cir. 1977).

NATURE OF CASE: Appeal of court order mandating compliance with administrative guidelines.

FACT SUMMARY: The Food and Drug Administration issued guidelines for proper processing of smoked whitefish, without disclosing the data upon which it based its decision and without commenting upon the necessity of the guidelines.

🏛 RULE OF LAW
Informal rulemaking must involve disclosure of relevant scientific data and statements concerning the need for the rule.

FACTS: The Food and Drug Administration (FDA) (P) adopted a series of guidelines for the prevention of botulism in smoked fish, prescribing time-temperature-salinity requirements. These regulations were applied to smoked whitefish, despite the fact that the regulations were commercially burdensome, and virtually no cases of botulism in whitefish had been reported. Nova Scotia Food Products Corp. (Nova Scotia) (D) made alternative suggestions. The FDA (P) promulgated the rules in question without disclosing the scientific data upon which it based its conclusions and issued no statements concerning the reasons for the rules' adoption. When Nova Scotia (D) failed to comply, the FDA (P) obtained a court injunction mandating compliance.

ISSUE: Must informal rulemaking involve disclosure of relevant scientific data and statements concerning the need for the rule?

HOLDING AND DECISION: (Gurfein, J.) Yes. Informal rulemaking must involve disclosure of relevant scientific data and statements concerning the need for the rule. While a court should not substitute its judgment for that of an agency's, it may pass upon whether or not the procedures used were proper. Where no issues of national security or trade secrets exist, it is not unreasonable to demand that an agency share its data with interested parties. It is also not too much for an agency to formulate clear reasons for its rules, as this helps to minimize arbitrariness and facilitates judicial review. Since these requisites were not adhered to in this instance, the district court compliance order must be vacated.

▶ ANALYSIS

The statute at issue here, as is usually the case in controversies involving administrative rulemaking, is 5 U.S.C. § 553. This section gives agencies broad informal rulemaking power. However, there are certain minimum procedures with which an agency must comply. Here, the FDA did not comply with subsection (c), which mandates that a concise statement accompany the rule.

■■■

Quicknotes

NOTICE AND COMMENT Informal rulemaking.

■■■

Vermont Yankee Nuclear Power Corp. v. Natural Resources Defense Council, Inc.

Nuclear power plant (D) v. Environmental group (P)

435 U.S. 519 (1978).

NATURE OF CASE: Appeal in connection with review of agency rulemaking procedure.

FACT SUMMARY: The Nuclear Regulatory Commission (D) promulgated a rule on nuclear wastes, but this was struck down on review because of alleged procedural defects.

🏛 RULE OF LAW
The adequacy of the record in an agency rulemaking proceeding is not correlated directly to the type of procedural devices employed but turns on whether the agency has followed the statutory mandate of the Administrative Procedure Act.

FACTS: In connection with a grant of a permit to build a nuclear power plant to Vermont Yankee Nuclear Power Corp. (Vermont Yankee) (D) and its receipt of an operating license therefor, an issue concerning disposal of toxic nuclear wastes arose. Although this issue was excluded from consideration in the Nuclear Regulatory Commission's (the Commission's) (D) hearings on the operating license, the Commission (D) subsequently promulgated a rule concerning the waste problem. National Resources Defense Council, Inc. (NRDC) (P) appealed from both the Commission's (D) adoption of the rule and its decision to grant Vermont Yankee's (D) license to the Court of Appeals for the District of Columbia Circuit. The court remanded the question of Vermont Yankee's (D) license for further proceedings. The court then invalidated the rulemaking proceedings despite the fact that it appeared that the agency employed all the procedures required by the Administrative Procedure Act. Vermont Yankee (D) argued that the Commission (D) may grant a license to operate a nuclear reactor without any consideration of waste disposal and fuel reprocessing, although the Commission (D) considered this issue includable in individual license proceedings. The rulemaking proceedings were reviewed on the basis of the record only.

ISSUE: Does the adequacy of the record in an agency rulemaking proceeding correlate directly to the type of procedural devices employed but turn on whether the agency has followed the statutory mandate of the Administrative Procedure Act?

HOLDING AND DECISION: (Rehnquist, J.) The adequacy of the record in an agency rulemaking proceeding is not correlated directly to the type of procedural devices employed but turns on whether the agency has followed the statutory mandate of the Administrative Procedure Act. Vermont Yankee's (D) contention fails because the Commission

(D) was well within its authority on the waste disposal and fuel reprocessing issue as they applied in individual license proceedings. However, the court of appeals was incorrect in its invalidation of the Commission's (D) rulemaking proceeding. Absent constitutional restraints or extremely compelling circumstances, the administrative agencies should be free to fashion their own rules of procedure and to pursue methods of inquiry capable of permitting them to discharge their duties. There are three compelling reasons why the agencies' discretion should be determinative. First, if courts continually review agency proceedings to determine whether the agency employed procedures which were what the court perceived to be the best or correct results, judicial review would be totally unpredictable. Second, the fact that the court looked only at the record and not at information available to the Commission (D) when it decided to structure the proceedings in a certain way is an example of Monday-morning-quarterbacking which would compel the agency to conduct all rulemaking proceedings with the full panoply of procedural devices normally associated only with adjudicatory hearings. Finally, and perhaps most importantly, this type of review misconceives the standard for judicial review of an agency rule; rulemaking need not be based solely on the transcript of a hearing. In fact, in a case like this, there need not be a formal hearing. Reversed and remanded.

▶ ANALYSIS

Executive Order 12044 concerned President Carter's directive to the agencies to "adopt procedures to improve existing and future regulations." 43 Fed. Reg. 12661. The order called for greater involvement by the public. This consisted, in part, of suggestions concerning published notices, conferences, hearings, and direct mailings. Gellhorn, W., Admin. Law, 203–204.

Quicknotes

5 U.S.C. § 553 Establishes minimum requirements of public rulemaking procedure.

JUDICIAL REVIEW The authority of the courts to review decisions, actions, or omissions committed by another agency or branch of government.

ADJUDICATORY PROCEEDING A hearing conducted by an administrative agency resulting in a final judgment regarding the rights of the parties involved.

Sierra Club v. Costle

Environmental group (P) v. Environmental Protection Agency (D)

657 F.2d 298 (D.C. Cir. 1981).

NATURE OF CASE: Appeal of certain coal combustion emission standards.

FACT SUMMARY: The Environmental Protection Agency (EPA) (D) adopted certain coal combustion emission standards following an informal rulemaking procedure wherein the EPA (D) entertained input following the official end of the comment period.

🏛 RULE OF LAW
When promulgating a rule under the 1977 Clean Air Act, the EPA may receive input following the close of the official comment period.

FACTS: In 1977, Congress enacted the Clean Air Act. One of the actions with which the Environmental Protection Agency (EPA) (D) was charged was to set reduction targets for emissions from coal combustion. When the EPA (D) failed to adopt such rules within one year, per statute, the Environmental Defense Fund (EDF) (P) and others brought suit. The EPA (D) eventually adopted rules including a limit of 1.2 lbs./Mbtu on emissions. The EPA (D) had considered standards as low as .55 lbs./Mbtu but did not adopt them due to concerns of economic hardship. In the period between the end of the comment period and rule promulgation, word of the possibility of the .55 standard was leaked, and numerous contacts, both written and oral, were made, including contacts by Congressmen and the White House. The EDF (P) appealed the rule, claiming that the postcomment period communications were improper. Most such comments had been placed in the record.

ISSUE: When promulgating a rule under the 1977 Clean Air Act, may the EPA receive input following the close of the official comment period?

HOLDING AND DECISION: (Wald, J.) Yes. When promulgating a rule under the 1977 Clean Air Act, the EPA (D) may receive input following the close of the official comment period. A decision of the EPA (D) under the Act may be overturned procedurally only if the errors were very serious and directly relevant to the outcome. "Ex parte" contacts such as occurred here may be improper for judicial proceedings, but in a political arena such as rulemaking this court cannot assume, in the absence of express language, that such contacts were to be forbidden. This is especially true when, as here, these contacts are put into the record. Having them in the record negates the argument that some "secret process" was occurring. The EDF (P) cannot point to any postcomment period document or meeting to which it did not have an opportunity to respond.

With all of this being considered, it cannot be said that serious error occurred here. Affirmed.

▶ ANALYSIS

Not all of the meetings that occurred here went into the official record. Some meetings between EPA (D) officials and White House officials did not. The court was of the opinion that the President does have an inherent right to monitor policy making in the executive branch.

Quicknotes

CLEAN AIR ACT, § 307 Requires certain content in the rulemaking record.

EX PARTE A proceeding commenced by one party without providing any opposing parties with notice or which is uncontested by an adverse party.

Association of National Advertisers, Inc. v. FTC

Trade group (P) v. Government agency (D)

627 F.2d 1151 (D.C. Cir. 1979).

NATURE OF CASE: Appeal from injunction forbidding agency chair from participating in television advertising rulemaking.

FACT SUMMARY: The Chairman of the Federal Trade Commission (D) declined to recuse himself from rulemaking concerning children's television advertising after he had taken a public stand on the issue.

🏛 RULE OF LAW
An agency member should be disqualified from decision making only when it is shown he has a closed mind on matters critical to the proceeding.

FACTS: The Federal Trade Commission (D) proposed regulations with respect to the advertising of various products on children's television. The Association of National Advertisers, Inc. (ANA) (P) requested that the chairman recuse himself because he had made oral and written pronouncements on the issue. The chairman declined to recuse himself. The ANA (P) filed suit in district court, seeking an injunction disqualifying the chairman from further participation. The court issued such an order.

ISSUE: Should an agency member be disqualified from decision-making only when it is shown he has a closed mind on matters critical to the proceeding?

HOLDING AND DECISION: (Tamm, J.) Yes. An agency member should be disqualified from decision-making only when it is shown he has a closed mind on matters critical to the proceeding. Rulemaking, unlike adjudication, is a political process, and it cannot be expected that rules will be made in a political vacuum. No one can seriously argue that decisions cannot be made by members of Congress who have set opinions prior to fact-finding, and where such power has been delegated, the only restrictions imposed are by due process, which requires only that the decision-maker consider contrary arguments. The ANA (P) failed to show that the chairman would not consider contrary arguments, and, hence, his disqualification was improper. Reversed.

CONCURRENCE: (Leventhal, J.) Unlike a judge, an administrative agent cannot set aside personal views of the desirability of laws or rules.

DISSENT: (MacKinnon, J.) Administrative agents do not have the same checks and balances that Congress does and should have stronger guarantees of impartiality placed on them.

▶ ANALYSIS

Administrative hearings and actions are supposed to be impartial, but as the court says, complete impartiality in the political process is neither possible nor desirable. The court here did not lay down clear guidelines as to what a plaintiff must prove to show impermissible bias. The burden would appear to be substantial.

■==■

Quicknotes

MAGNUSON-MOSS ACT, § 18 Requires commission to conduct hearings to resolve disputed hearings.

■==■

Securities & Exchange Commission v. Chenery Corp.

Parties not identified.

332 U.S. 194 (1947).

NATURE OF CASE: Appeal from an administrative order.

FACT SUMMARY: The Securities & Exchange Commission (SEC) (D) withheld approval of a corporate reorganization plan in which the Chenery Corporation (P) was a participant. The Supreme Court refused to sustain the SEC's (D) order, but on remand, the SEC (D) again declined to permit operation of the proposed plan, although on the second occasion the SEC (D) cited different reasons for its order.

🏛 RULE OF LAW
Even when confronted with novel issues, agencies may make adjudications which are binding upon the parties to the controversy rather than announcing rules of prospective application only.

FACTS: A reorganization plan for the Federal Water Service Company (Federal), a holding company registered under the Public Utility Company Act of 1935, was submitted to the Securities and Exchange Commission (SEC) (D) for approval. Officers (P), directors (P), and controlling shareholders (P) of Federal (including the named defendant, Chenery Corporation) purchased a substantial amount of Federal's preferred stock, and under the reorganization plan this stock was to be converted into common stock in a new corporation. For this reason, the plan was unacceptable to the SEC (D), which ruled that the directors (P), etc., were fiduciaries and therefore not entitled to deal in securities of the company. The SEC's (D) order was reversed by the court upon a finding that the decision lacked legal precedent. On remand, however, the SEC (D) reached the same result, this time predicating its order on the fact that it was the product of agency expertise. Chenery Corporation (P) again sought judicial review, contending that, inasmuch as the SEC (D) had acknowledged that no precedent existed for its order, it should proceed only by announcing a rule of prospective application and not by rendering an adjudication which would bind the parties to the present controversy.

ISSUE: Must agencies deal with novel issues by promulgating rules of prospective application only, or may they render adjudications which are binding upon the parties to an actual controversy as well?

HOLDING AND DECISION: (Murphy, J.) Yes. Agencies confronted with novel issues of law may announce rules of prospective application, but they may also render adjudications which are binding upon the parties to such controversies as are presented to the agency. Although the application of a ruling to a current controversy may present a retroactivity problem, the detriment of such an effect must be balanced against the agency's need to reach a satisfactory resolution of the case before it. Thus, in the present, where the SEC's (D) general experience and the facts of the case support a conclusion that the Chenery Corporation (P) should have been precluded from converting its preferred stock into common stock of a new corporation, any problem of retroactivity is outweighed by the necessity of prohibiting the proscribed conduct in the immediate case. Accordingly, the SEC (D) was not required in this case to proceed by prospective rule only, although such a procedure may ordinarily be preferable to ad hoc determinations.

DISSENT: (Jackson, J.) The Court's approval of such administrative authoritarianism undervalues and belittles the place of law, even in the system of administrative justice.

▶ ANALYSIS

Although the courts apparently prefer that agencies proceed by general rulemaking rather than by ad hoc case-by-case adjudication, the latter procedure is clearly countenanced by the courts. And in rendering its decisions on an ad hoc basis, agencies are permitted a freer hand than are courts themselves. For instance, inconsistent decisions rendered by an agency may not be attacked on that basis, unless the inconsistency is so glaring as to constitute an abuse of agency discretion. And rules of res judicata have traditionally been relaxed in the agency context, although there is an apparent trend toward recognizing res judicata principles as essential elements of agency decision making.

■■■

Quicknotes

AD HOC DECISION A decision made for a specific purpose.

RES JUDICATA The rule of law that a final judgment by a court precludes subsequent litigation between the parties regarding the same cause of action.

■■■

Morton v. Ruiz

Bureau of Indian Affairs (D) v. Native American (P)

415 U.S. 199 (1974).

NATURE OF CASE: Application for general assistance benefits.

FACT SUMMARY: Ruiz (P), a Papago Indian and United States citizen, was denied general assistance benefits because he did not live on a reservation.

🏛 RULE OF LAW
Before an agency may extinguish the entitlement of potential beneficiaries, it must comply with its own internal procedures.

FACTS: The Bureau of Indian Affairs (BIA) (D) deemed that Indians would not be eligible for general assistance benefits if they did not live on a reservation. Ruiz (P), a Papago Indian and United States citizen, was denied general assistance benefits because he did not live on a reservation but resided with his wife in an Indian community 15 miles from a reservation. The BIA (D) did not publish its eligibility requirements for general assistance in the federal register. This was the case even though the BIA (D) declared in its manual that eligibility requirements for benefits were to be published. Ruiz (P) utilized in full his administrative remedies and then brought suit in the district court, which dismissed the action. The court of appeals reversed, and the U.S. Supreme Court granted certiorari.

ISSUE: Before an agency may extinguish the entitlement of potential beneficiaries, must it comply with its own internal procedures?

HOLDING AND DECISION: (Blackmun, J.) Yes. Before an agency may extinguish the entitlement of potential beneficiaries, it must comply with its own internal procedures. The congressional intent is not to exclude Indians not living on the reservation. The congressional appropriation was intended to cover welfare services at least to those Indians residing on or near the reservation. Although the BIA (D) has the power to create reasonable classifications, no matter how rational or consistent with congressional intent a particular decision might be, the determination of eligibility cannot be made on an ad hoc basis by the dispenser of the funds. Here, the BIA (D) chose not to publish its eligibility requirements for general assistance in the federal register. The only official manifestation of its policy is in the manual. Before the BIA (D) may extinguish the entitlement of these otherwise eligible beneficiaries, it must comply, at a minimum, with its own internal procedures. The BIA (D) must promulgate eligibility requirements according to established procedures. Affirmed and remanded.

▶ ANALYSIS

According to Professor Fuchs, this case stands partly for the proposition that "limitations on eligibility may not be newly imposed case by case, even on the basis of reasoned opinions, because the limitations must be made known in advance to persons adversely affected by them." Furthermore, Fuchs says that the development of criteria which seems to conflict with the statutory mandate is a power which is hard to regulate. Moreover, this power is an extremely wide one. Gellhorn, W., Admin. Law, 239.

■≡■

CHAPTER 6

Government Information Acquisition and Disclosure

Quick Reference Rules of Law

University of Pennsylvania v. Equal Employment Opportunity Commission

College (D) v. Governmental agency (P)

493 U.S. 182 (1990).

NATURE OF CASE: Appeal from grant of order to enforce subpoena.

FACT SUMMARY: In the Equal Employment Opportunity Commission's (P) subpoena enforcement action against the University of Pennsylvania (D), the court of appeals, affirming the district court's decision, compelled the University of Pennsylvania (D) to produce tenure review materials that were relevant to a racial discrimination charge brought against it.

🏛 RULE OF LAW
Unless otherwise specified by statute, the Equal Employment Opportunity Commission may obtain relevant evidence in its investigative efforts.

FACTS: In the Equal Employment Opportunity Commission's (EEOC's) (P) subpoena enforcement action against the University of Pennsylvania (University) (D), the Third Circuit Court of Appeals, affirming the district court's decision, enforced the EEOC's (P) subpoena against the University (D), requiring it to produce tenure review materials that were relevant to a faculty member's racial discrimination charges against it. The University (D) appealed.

ISSUE: Unless otherwise specified by statute, may the EEOC obtain relevant evidence in its investigative efforts?

HOLDING AND DECISION: (Blackmun, J.) Yes. Unless otherwise specified by statute, the EEOC (P) may obtain relevant evidence in its investigative efforts. This rule is consistent with the Equal Employment Opportunity Act's grant to the EEOC (P) of a broad discretionary privilege to sift through relevant evidence. The Act is qualified, however, by Fed. R. Evid. 501, which establishes a witness' privilege to withhold relevant evidence from the EEOC (P) where important constitutional or societal interests are somewhat infringed upon. However, where it appears that Congress has considered the relevant competing concerns but has not provided such a privilege, an infringement upon these interests is justified. In the instant case, since disclosure of the relevant tenure review materials would not infringe upon important societal or constitutional interests, the EEOC's (P) order to enforce its subpoena was properly granted. Affirmed.

▌ ANALYSIS

There is persistent controversy in higher education as to whether peer review materials that are part of tenure and promotion processes should be made available to faculty candidates. Many institutions, like the University of Pennsylvania (D), prefer confidentiality on the ground that disclosure of peer review materials would chill candid appraisals and compromise professional relationships. Other institutions, believing that anonymity invites abuse, deem an "open file" system to be fairer to faculty candidates and regard the availability of review materials to the candidate to be an important check on their quality and accuracy.

■═■

Quicknotes

FEDERAL RULE OF EVIDENCE 501 Provides that privilege principles shall be based on common law.

TITLE VII Prohibits unlawful discrimination against individuals based on race or gender.

■═■

Marshall v. Barlow's, Inc.

OSHA (P) v. Business (D)

436 U.S. 307 (1978).

NATURE OF CASE: Appeal in connection with an attempted administrative search.

FACT SUMMARY: Barlow (D), the proprietor of Barlow's, Inc., refused entry to an official attempting an inspection because the official did not have a warrant.

🏛 RULE OF LAW
An administrative search under the Occupational Safety and Health Act (OSHA) may not be conducted without a warrant.

FACTS: Barlow (D) refused entry to an OSHA inspector attempting an inspection of his business because the official did not have a warrant. Marshall (P), the Secretary of Labor, petitioned the district court to issue an order compelling Barlow (D) to admit the inspector. The order was issued, but Barlow (D) again refused the inspector admission. Barlow (D) sought his own injunctive relief against the warrantless searches. The district court held for Barlow (D).

ISSUE: May an administrative search under OSHA be conducted without a warrant?

HOLDING AND DECISION: (White, J.) No. An administrative search under OSHA may not be conducted without a warrant. This is not to say that the probable cause standards in criminal cases apply. For purposes of an administrative search such as this, probable cause justifying the issuance of a warrant may be based not only on specific evidence of an existing violation but also on a showing that reasonable legislative or administrative standards for conducting an inspection are satisfied with respect to a particular place of business. Affirmed.

DISSENT: (Stevens, J.) The Warrant Clause has no application to routine, regulatory inspections of commercial premises.

▶ ANALYSIS

Justice White also wrote the decisions in *Camara v. Munmicipal Court*, 387 U.S. 523 (1967) and *See v. Seattle*, 387 U.S. 541 (1967).. Those two cases are the starting point in determining the validity of an administrative search. Both cases held that the Warrant Clause applied and controlled. Gellhorn, W., Admin. Law, at 541.

Quicknotes

FOURTH AMENDMENT Provides that persons be secure as to their person and private belongings against unreasonable searches and seizures.

NLRB v. Sears, Roebuck & Co.

Government agency (D) v. Employer (P)

421 U.S. 132 (1975).

NATURE OF CASE: Appeal of court order compelling disclosure of documents.

FACT SUMMARY: Sears, Roebuck & Co. (P) obtained an order compelling disclosure of National Labor Relations Board (D) Appeals and Advice Memoranda.

🏛 RULE OF LAW
National Labor Relations Board Appeals and Advice Memoranda upholding a decision not to file a complaint are subject to Freedom of Information Act disclosure, but those reversing such a decision are not.

FACTS: Regional officers of the National Labor Relations Board (NLRB) (D) had decision-making authority to issue an unfair labor practices complaint upon an interested person's application. If such an application were denied, the applicant had the option of appealing to the central NLRB (D) office. On advice of general counsel, the NLRB (D) would either uphold the decision not to file or reverse it. Sears, Roebuck & Co. (Sears) (P) applied, under the Freedom of Information Act (FOIA), for disclosure of certain Appeals and Advice Memoranda relevant to Sears (P). The NLRB (D) refused, contending that such memoranda were exempt from disclosure. Sears (P) obtained a court order compelling disclosure.

ISSUE: Are NLRB Appeals and Advice Memoranda subject to FOIA disclosure?

HOLDING AND DECISION: (White, J.) NLRB Appeals and Advise Memoranda upholding a decision not to file a complaint are subject to disclosure, but those reversing such a decision are not. Exempted from FOIA disclosure are intra-agency documents which reflect the thought processes of agency general counsel. This provision is analogous to the attorney work product privilege in civil discovery. Memoranda which pertain to a decision to file a complaint invariably contain the thought processes of general counsel and are exempt from the Act. Memoranda which relate to a decision not to file a complaint basically reflect the ending of a case and for that reason is much like final orders. Final orders are not exempt. For these reasons, the district court order is reversed as to those memoranda reflecting a decision to file a complaint.

▶ *ANALYSIS*

The statutory language of the relevant exception to the FOIA is somewhat vague. It had been believed that it might apply to almost all agency-authored documents. As the present case made clear, however, it will not apply to documentation pertaining to final orders.

■■■

Quicknotes

FREEDOM OF INFORMATION ACT Enables courts to enjoin agencies from withholding records and to order production.

FREEDOM OF INFORMATION ACT § 552 Expressly defines records which must be made available to public.

■■■

NLRB v. Robbins Tire & Rubber Co.

Government agency (D) v. Employer (P)

437 U.S. 214 (1978).

NATURE OF CASE: Appeal of court order compelling disclosure of witness statements prior to a National Labor Relations Board hearing.

FACT SUMMARY: The National Labor Relations Board (D) denied a request for the disclosure of witness statements prior to an unfair labor practices hearing concerning Robbins Tire and Rubber Co. (P).

🏛 RULE OF LAW
Witness statements do not have to be disclosed under the Freedom of Information Act prior to a National Labor Relations Board hearing.

FACTS: Robbins Tire & Rubber Co. (Robbins) (P), subject to an unfair labor practices complaint, sought disclosure under the Freedom of Information Act (FOIA) of witness statements. The National Labor Relations Board (NLRB) (D) refused, stating that the statements were exempt from discovery in that they were investigatory records whose disclosure would interfere with agency enforcement proceedings. Robbins (P) obtained a court order compelling disclosure, and the court of appeals affirmed.

ISSUE: Do witness statements have to be disclosed under the Freedom of Information Act prior to an NLRB hearing?

HOLDING AND DECISION: (Marshall, J.) No. Witness statements do not have to be disclosed under the FOIA prior to an NLRB hearing. The FOIA specifically exempted from disclosure investigative materials whose disclosure would interfere with enforcement proceedings. The question, therefore, is whether disclosure here would interfere with the hearing. It seems clear that witness disclosure could lead to witness intimidation on both sides. Also, Congress has created a delicately balanced system for resolving labor disputes, and the Court is not inclined to introduce a major change absent specific legislative intent. Finally, the FOIA was intended to be a general avenue for popular oversight of governmental action, not a litigation discovery device. Reversed.

DISSENT: (Powell, J.) The agency in question should have to prove potential interference on a case-by-case basis.

▶ ANALYSIS

A point seemingly added by the Court almost as an afterthought is of potentially great import in this area. The FOIA, says the Court, was not meant to be a discovery device of litigants. If the Court were to cite this rationale in all FOIA cases, it would seem that the scope of the FOIA could be curtailed considerably.

■═■

Quicknotes

FREEDOM OF INFORMATION ACT, EXEMPTION 7 Exempts investigatory records prepared for law-enforcement purposes.

■═■

Chrysler Corp. v. Brown

Auto manufacturer (P) v. Department of Labor (D)

441 U.S. 281 (1979).

NATURE OF CASE: Appeal of court order mandating disclosure of certain documents.

FACT SUMMARY: Chrysler Corp. (P) contended that certain documents pertaining to it held by the government fell outside the Freedom of Information Act and, therefore, could not be disclosed pursuant to unrelated regulations.

🏛 RULE OF LAW
The Freedom of Information Act does not give rise to a private right to prevent disclosure of documents pursuant to unrelated regulations.

FACTS: Pursuant to Executive Order, Chrysler Corp. (P) had to prepare certain reports giving the status of Chrysler's (P) compliance with federal affirmative action programs. The Executive Order and Regulations of the Department of Labor (D) allowed for public inspection of these records. The Deptartment of Labor (D) informed Chrysler (P) that a request for some of these records had been made. Chrysler (P) argued that the records contained trade secrets and, therefore, fell under Exemption 4 of the Freedom of Information Act (FOIA). The court of appeals held the documents subject to disclosure.

ISSUE: Does the FOIA give rise to a private right to prevent disclosure of documents pursuant to unrelated regulations?

HOLDING AND DECISION: (Rehnquist, J.) No. The FOIA does not give rise to a private right to prevent disclosure of documents pursuant to unrelated regulations. The FOIA, by its terms, is exclusively a disclosure statute. This is borne out by its provisions for judicial review, which allow a court to order disclosure but say nothing about withholding disclosure. Also, legislative history makes it clear that the FOIA was designed to create an avenue for disclosure pursuant to other laws. [The Court went on to hold that the Trade Secrets Act may prevent disclosure and remanded to the court of appeals for consideration of this issue.]

▶ ANALYSIS

This was what had been labeled a "reverse FOIA" suit. Suppliers of information to the government had argued, as did Chrysler (P), that disclosure broader than that allowed by the FOIA was impermissible. The argument was that the FOIA had superseded all other disclosure rules. This decision put that argument to rest.

Quicknotes

FREEDOM OF INFORMATION ACT, EXEMPTION 4 Exempts trade secrets and privileges or confidential financial information from disclosure.

■═■

Department of Defense v. Federal Labor Relations Authority

Government employer (P) v. Government agency (D)

510 U.S. 487 (1994).

NATURE OF CASE: Appeal from judgment granting access to the home addresses of federal employees.

FACT SUMMARY: Two labor unions filed charges with the Federal Labor Relations Authority (D) to force the Department of Defense (P) and several other federal agencies (P) to divulge the home addresses of the agencies' (D) workers.

🏛 RULE OF LAW
In evaluating whether a request for information lies within the scope of a Freedom of Information Act exemption, a court must balance the public interest in disclosure against the interest Congress intended the exemption to protect.

FACTS: Two labor unions requested that the Department of Defense (DOD) (P) and other federal agencies (P) provide a listing of the names and home addresses of those employees belonging to bargaining units represented by the unions. DOD (P) supplied employee names and work stations, but refused to release their home addresses. The unions filed an unfair labor practices claim with the Federal Labor Relations Authority (the Authority) (D), claiming a federal labor law statute required DOD (P) to divulge the addresses. DOD (P) claimed that disclosure of the home addresses was prohibited by the Privacy Act. After hearings, the Authority (D) ordered the home addresses to be provided. DOD (P) filed for judicial review of the Authority's (D) orders in federal court. The Fifth Circuit enforced the orders, concluding that the Freedom of Information Act (FOIA) required disclosure. DOD (P) appealed, and the Supreme Court granted review.

ISSUE: In evaluating whether a request for information lies within the scope of an FOIA exemption, must a court balance the public interest in disclosure against the interest Congress intended the exemption to protect?

HOLDING AND DECISION: (Thomas, J.) Yes. In evaluating whether a request for information lies within the scope of an FOIA exemption, a court must balance the public interest in disclosure against the interest Congress intended the exemption to protect. Under federal labor law, agencies must provide unions with any data necessary for collective-bargaining purposes to the extent that furnishing such information is not prohibited by law. Here, the requested employee records are covered under the Privacy Act. The Privacy Act bars disclosure unless disclosure would be required under the FOIA. In turn, FOIA requires the release of the addresses, unless they fall within an exception to FOIA—specifically, Exemption 6, which prohibits disclosure of personnel files constituting an unwarranted invasion of personal privacy. To determine whether Exemption 6 applies, a court must balance the public interest in disclosure against the protected interest of the individual's privacy, and the only public interest in disclosure is whether the requested information significantly contributes to public understanding of government operations or activities. Here, the requested information contributes nothing to public understanding of the government. Hence, the privacy interest outweighs the public interest. Reversed.

▶ ANALYSIS

The Privacy Act restricts third party access to personal information contained in government files. In short, the law assures that an individual's personal information is not released to third parties without their knowledge and consent. The Privacy Act also permits individuals to challenge the accuracy of information about them contained in government files. As such, the Privacy Act creates a presumption against disclosing records, unless the party requesting access is the subject of the records in question.

■▬■

Quicknotes

FREEDOM OF INFORMATION ACT, EXEMPTION 6 Excludes personnel and medical files.

PRIVACY ACT Protects from disclosure information that involves personal private matters.

■▬■

Suits to Review Administrative Action

Quick Reference Rules of Law

Citizens to Preserve Overton Park, Inc. v. Volpe

Citizens' group (P) v. Department of Transportation (D)

401 U.S. 402 (1971).

NATURE OF CASE: Suit to set aside administrative action.

FACT SUMMARY: A group of concerned citizens (P) sued the Secretary of Transportation (D), challenging his decision to construct a highway through a public park.

> ## 🏛 RULE OF LAW
> When reviewing administrative decisions which are not supported by formal factual findings, the courts should determine the scope of the appropriate official's authority, whether that authority was abused, and whether all applicable procedural requisites have been observed.

FACTS: The Citizens to Preserve Overton Park, Inc. (Citizens) (P) sued Secretary Volpe (D) of the Department of Transportation. He was accused of violating the Department of Transportation Act and the Federal-Aid Highway Act by approving plans to construct a six-lane highway through Overton Park, a popular recreation site. The Citizens (P) assailed Volpe (D) for his failure to state the factual findings upon which he based his decision. The Citizens (P) also alleged Volpe (D) failed to explain why he believed, as required by statute, that no feasible alternative location was available and that all possible steps had been taken to minimize harm to the park. The Citizens (P) sought to have Volpe's (D) decision nullified, but the district court granted the Secretary's (D) motion for summary judgment, basing its ruling on the contents of affidavits which had been prepared specifically in response to the litigation. The court of appeals affirmed, but the Supreme Court granted a stay and agreed to review the decisions below. On appeal, the Citizens (P) sought either a de novo review of the Secretary's (D) decision or application of the substantial evidence test.

ISSUE: In reviewing administrative decisions which are unembellished by formal findings of fact, must the court confine its evaluation to the contents of affidavits submitted by the agency at trial?

HOLDING AND DECISION: (Marshall, J.) No. The reviewing court must determine the scope of the duties of the official involved in a decision, whether he abused the authority vested in him, and whether in arriving at his decision he observed all applicable procedural requisites. The case is not one in which the court may appropriately undertake a de novo review of the Secretary's (D) decision since it presents neither a circumstance in which an adjudicatory proceeding was supported by inadequate fact-finding procedures nor one in which new issues are raised in a proceeding to enforce nonadjudicatory agency action. Likewise, the substantial evidence test should not be applied to the Secretary's (D) action since his decision was neither the product of a public adjudicatory hearing nor an exercise of the Secretary's (D) rulemaking function. However, the fact that de novo review and application of the substantial evidence test are both inappropriate in this case does not mean that the Citizens (P) are not entitled to a thoroughgoing review of the Secretary's (D) actions. The applicable statutes clearly mandate that the Secretary (D) shall act only when all effective alternative sites for highway construction have been ruled out and, even then, only after taking all available steps to minimize harm to the chosen location. The Citizens (P) were entitled to a review of the Secretary's (D) deliberative processes, which took account of more evidence than that which was contained in the affidavits upon which the courts below based their decisions. Therefore, it is necessary that this case be remanded for reconsideration, based on broader evidence than that heretofore evaluated, of whether the Secretary (D) observed the required procedure of investigating alternative routes and insuring only minimal harm to Overton Park. In reviewing the Secretary's (D) decision, the district court, if it wishes, may even undertake the unusual procedure of requiring the appropriate administrative officials to reveal the thought processes by which they arrived at their conclusions. Although the district court need not adopt this drastic course, should it choose to, it may resort to this procedure as a means of compensating for the lack of any factual findings upon which to predicate its decision.

▷ ANALYSIS

The principal significance of *Citizens to Preserve Overton Park, Inc. v. Volpe* rests in its concern with insuring that judicial review of administrative decisions will be meaningful. To that end, the *Overton Park* Court countenanced the extraordinary procedure of probing the deliberative processes of administrative officials. It seems clear that the provisions of the Administrative Procedure Act calling for judicial review of administrative determinations cannot be implemented in the absence of a record sufficient to accommodate review and that when such a record is absent the courts must choose between ordering its compilation or undertaking their own review de novo.

■■■

Quicknotes

DE NOVO The review of a lower court decision by an appellate court, which is hearing the case as if it had not been previously heard and as if no judgment had been rendered.

ADJUDICATORY PROCEEDING A hearing conducted by an administrative agency resulting in a final judgment regarding the rights of the parties involved.

■■■

Chevron, U.S.A., Inc. v. Natural Resources Defense Council, Inc.

Oil company (D) v. Environmental group (P)

467 U.S. 837 (1984).

NATURE OF CASE: Appeal from decision setting aside EPA regulations.

FACT SUMMARY: Chevron, U.S.A., Inc. (D) appealed from a decision setting aside Environmental Protection Agency (EPA) regulations relating to the interpretation of the term "stationary source," contending that the EPA's regulations should have been upheld since they were based on a reasonable construction of the term "stationary source."

🏛 RULE OF LAW
Absent clear legislative intent on statutory construction, judicial review of an agency's construction of a statute is limited to a determination of whether it is a permissible construction of the statute.

FACTS: The amended Clean Air Act required no-attainment states, i.e., states originally required to meet certain air pollution standards under the unamended Clean Air Act, to establish a permit program regulating new or modified stationary sources of air pollution. The Environmental Protection Agency (EPA) promulgated regulations interpreting the term "stationary source" so as to allow states to treat all of the pollution-emitting devices within the same industrial group as though encased within the same bubble. The court of appeals set aside the regulations upon petition by the Natural Resources Defense Council, Inc. (P) as contrary to law, finding the bubble concept inappropriate in programs designed to improve air quality. Chevron, U.S.A., Inc. (D) appealed, contending the regulations were based upon a reasonable construction of the term "stationary source."

ISSUE: Absent clear legislative intent on statutory construction, is judicial review of an agency's construction of a statute limited to a determination of whether it is a permissible construction of the statute?

HOLDING AND DECISION: (Stevens, J.) Yes. Absent clear legislative intent on statutory construction, judicial review of an agency's construction of a statute is limited to a determination of whether it is a permissible construction of the statute. The court may not substitute its own statutory construction for a reasonable interpretation made by an agency. The legislative history behind the EPA regulations makes no specific comment on the permissibility of the bubble concept but discusses the accommodation of the economic interest in capital improvement and environmental concerns. The EPA has consistently interpreted the term "stationary source" flexibly. It is the court of appeals that has applied a static definition to the term. The EPA's regulations represent a reasonable accommodation among congressionally delineated interests and should have been upheld. Reversed.

▶ ANALYSIS

The first step in the process is to determine legislative intent. If the legislature gives clear and unambiguous guidance as to how to interpret any statutory term, the agency does not have discretion to interpret but must adopt regulations that enforce the express intention of Congress.

Quicknotes

JUDICIAL REVIEW The authority of the courts to review decisions, actions, or omissions committed by another agency or branch of government.

CLEAN AIR ACT Required certain states to establish a permit program for stationary sources of air pollution.

United States v. Mead Corp.

Federal government (D) v. Corporation (P)

533 U.S. 218 (2001).

NATURE OF CASE: Appeal in a tariff assessment action.

FACT SUMMARY: Mead Corporation (P) was assessed a tariff on its day planners, and it protested to Customs. Customs issued a ruling letter explaining why Mead (P) was assessed a tariff.

🏛 **RULE OF LAW**
A tariff classification ruling by the United States Customs Service does not deserve judicial deference.

FACTS: Mead Corporation (D) imports "day planners." The tariff schedule in regards to day planners is regulated by the Harmonized Tariff Schedule of the U.S. (the Schedule), which subjects day planners to a tariff of 4.0 percent. Until 1993, when Customs issued a Headquarters ruling letter classifying Mead's day planners as "Diaries . . . bound," day planners had been duty-free. In response to Mead's protest of the reclassification, Customs Headquarters issued a new letter, never published, and discussed the two definitions of diary from the dictionary; it concluded that the definition reflects commercial usage. As for the definition of "bound," Customs Headquarters concluded that "bound" meant "reinforcements or fittings of metal, plastics, etc." In the Schedule, Congress had conferred upon Customs the power to issue regulations to establish procedures for the issuance of binding rulings prior to the entry of the merchandise concerned and to disseminate information necessary to secure uniformity. A ruling letter represents the official position of the Customs Service with respect to a particular transaction or issue described therein. Since ruling letters respond to transactions of the moment, they are not subject to notice and comment before being issued, and although they may be published, they need only be made available for pubic inspection. In addition, the ruling has no bearing on nonparties to the transaction at issue. Forty-six different Customs offices issue 10,000 to 15,000 ruling letters per year. The court of appeals ruled that Customs ruling letters do not fall within *Chevron, U.S.A., Inc. v. Natural Resources Defense Council, Inc.*, 467 U.S. 837 (1984).

ISSUE: Does a tariff classification ruling by the United States Customs Service deserve judicial deference?

HOLDING AND DECISION: (Souter, J.) No. A tariff classification ruling by the United States Customs Service does not deserve judicial deference. A tariff classification has no claim to judicial deference under *Chevron* because there is no indication that Congress intended such a ruling to carry the force of law; under *Skidmore v. Swift & Co.*, 323 U.S. 134 (1944), however, the ruling is eligible to claim respect according to its persuasiveness. On the face of the statute, there is no congressional intent to give Customs classification rulings the force of law. In addition, there is in the agency's practice no indication that Customs ever set out with a lawmaking pretense in mind when it undertook to make such classifications. Moreover, the amendments to the statute don't reveal any new congressional objective of treating classification decisions generally as rulemaking with force of law. Furthermore, the authorization for classification rulings, and Customs practice in making them, present a case far removed not only from the notice-and-comment process but from any other circumstances reasonably suggesting that Congress ever thought of classification rulings as deserving the deference claimed for them here. The Customs ruling at issue here fails to qualify for deference under *Chevron*, although the possibility that it deserves some deference under *Skidmore* means the case is to be vacated.

DISSENT: (Scalia, J.) Established jurisprudence states that a reasonable agency application of an ambiguous statutory provision should be sustained, because Congress gives the agency discretion as to how to resolve the ambiguity, so long as it represents the agency's authoritative interpretation. In this case, therefore, deference should be given to the interpretation the Customs Service has given to the statute it is charged with enforcing, and the judgment of the court of appeals should be reversed. The majority opinion states that this ambiguity, however, is to be resolved by the courts and not the agencies; therefore, the practical effect of the majority's rule is confusion, an increase in informal rulemaking, and the exclusion of large portions of statutory law. The weight it gives to *Skidmore*, which is a statement of the obvious—"A judge should take into account the well-considered views of expert observers"—will lead to uncertainty.

▶ **ANALYSIS**

This case demonstrates that the majority of the Court didn't want to take an all-or-nothing approach in deferring to administrative agencies but preferred to support a variety of forms for such deference.

■═■

Quicknotes

TARIFF Duty or tax imposed on articles imported into the United States.

■═■

NLRB v. Hearst Publications

Government agency (P) v. Publishing employer (D)

322 U.S. 111 (1944).

NATURE OF CASE: Appeal from reversal of a National Labor Relations Board action seeking enforcement order.

FACT SUMMARY: Hearst Publications, Inc. (Hearst) (D) sought review of a decision of the National Labor Relations Board (P) ordering Hearst (D) to bargain with a local union of newsboys.

RULE OF LAW
A reviewing court must accept an agency's initial specific application of a broad statutory term when the agency makes the initial determination.

FACTS: These cases arise from the refusal of Hearst Publications, Inc. (Hearst) (D) to bargain collectively with a union representing newsboys who distributed its papers on the streets of Los Angeles. The proceedings before the National Labor Relations Board (Board) (P) were begun with the filing of four petitions for investigation and certification by Los Angeles Newsboys Local Industrial Union No. 75. Hearings were held after which the Board (P) made findings of fact and concluded that the regular full-time newsboys selling each paper were employees within the Act. The Board (P) ordered elections. At these elections, the union was selected as the newsboys' representative. Hearst (D) refused to bargain with the union. Thereupon proceedings were instituted, and the Board (P) ordered Hearst (D) to cease and desist from violating the Act and to bargain collectively with the union. Upon Hearst's (D) petitions for review and the Board's (P) petitions for enforcement, the court of appeals set aside the Board's (P) orders. Rejecting the Board's (P) analysis, the court independently examined whether the newsboys were employees within the Act, decided that the statute imported common law standards to determine that question, and held the newsboys were not employees. The Board (P) appealed.

ISSUE: Must a reviewing court accept an agency's initial specific application of a broad statutory term when the agency makes the initial determination?

HOLDING AND DECISION: (Rutledge, J.) Yes. A reviewing court must accept an agency's initial specific application of a broad statutory term when the agency makes the initial determination. Undoubtedly questions of statutory interpretation, especially when arising in the first instance in judicial proceedings, are for the courts to resolve, giving appropriate weight to the judgment of those whose special duty it is to administer the questioned statute. But where the question is one of specific application of a broad statutory term in a proceeding in which the agency administering the statute must determine it initially, the reviewing court's function is limited. It must accept the agency's determination if it has warrant in the record and a reasonable basis in law. In this case, the Board (P) found that the newsboys work continuously and regularly, rely upon their earnings for the support of themselves and their families, and have their total wages influenced by the publishers, who dictate their buying and selling prices, fix their markets, and control their supply of papers. The Board (P) concluded that the newsboys are employees within the meaning of the Act. The record sustains the Board's (P) findings, and there is ample basis in the law for its conclusion. Reversed.

DISSENT: (Roberts, J.) The task of defining "employee" within the meaning of the Act is a judicial function. Congress obviously intended that term to be accorded the common and general national definition which it enjoys. The court of appeals' application of that definition should not be disturbed.

ANALYSIS

According to Professor Schwartz, "a finding of employment such as that at issue in *Crowell v. Benson*, 285 U.S. 22 (1932), or *Hearst* involves both factual and legal elements. The agency must first find the underlying facts about the people involved. But that alone does not answer the question of whether they are employees. The agency must now determine whether the legal concept of employment in the enabling statute applies to the fact pattern found in the given case. The agency finding is not merely that certain 'facts' are true, but also that they sum up into the legal conclusion of employment."

Quicknotes

EMPLOYEE AT WILL An employee who works pursuant to the agreement that either he or his employer may terminate the employment relationship at any time and for any cause.

INDEPENDENT CONTRACTOR A party undertaking a particular assignment for another who retains control over the manner in which it is executed.

NATIONAL LABOR RELATIONS ACT Guarantees employees the right to engage in collective bargaining, and regulates labor unions.

NATIONAL LABOR RELATIONS BOARD An agency established pursuant to the National Labor Relations Act for the purpose of prohibiting unfair labor practices by employers and unions.

Industrial Union Department v. American Petroleum Institute

Parties not identified.

448 U.S. 607 (1980).

NATURE OF CASE: Appeal of invalidation of Occupational Safety and Health Administration work safety rules.

FACT SUMMARY: The Occupational Safety and Health Administration (D) adopted a rule mandating that benzene concentrations in the workplace had to be minimized to the greatest extent technologically possible.

🏛 RULE OF LAW

Before the Occupational Safety and Health Administration can promulgate health or safety standards, it must make a finding that significant risks are present and can be eliminated or lessened by a change in practices.

FACTS: The Occupational Safety and Health Act of 1970 (the Act) created the Occupational Safety and Health Administration (OSHA) (D), which was charged with insuring that industry provided healthful places of employment. Part of OSHA's (D) duties included prescribing maximum safe levels of exposure to toxins. With respect to carcinogens, OSHA (D) adopted the policy that any exposure was unhealthful and mandated that such exposure be the minimum that technology could provide. OSHA (D) adopted a rule mandating that benzene, a carcinogen, could not exist in workplaces in concentrations greater than 1 ppm. No substantial evidence existed that exposure to 10 ppm caused more cancer. Implementing the rule would cost industry over $1 billion. The rule was challenged as in excess of OSHA's (D) authority. The Fifth Circuit so held and invalidated the rule.

ISSUE: Before OSHA can promulgate health or safety standards, must it make a finding that significant risks are present and can be eliminated by a change in practices?

HOLDING AND DECISION: (Stevens, J.) Yes. Before OSHA (D) can promulgate health or safety standards, it must make a finding that significant risks are present and can be eliminated by a change in practices. In the absence of express delegation, it cannot be assumed that the Act granted to OSHA (D) sweeping authority to make sweeping changes in industry without finding that such changes are reasonably related to the agency's goal. Further, it must be concluded that OSHA's (D) mandate is to eliminate unreasonable risks, not all risks. Therefore, before OSHA (D) can specify a certain level of toxic exposure, it must show that higher levels are unreasonably dangerous. Here, no such finding was made. OSHA (D) simply assumed that no level of exposure was safe, without evidence to support this premise. Such a broad delegation of power cannot be assumed in the Act. Affirmed.

CONCURRENCE: (Powell, J.) The Act requires that OSHA (D) balance economic considerations with health concerns.

CONCURRENCE: (Rehnquist, J.) The issues here are of such import that only Congress should decide them.

DISSENT: (Marshall, J.) The findings of OSHA (D) were far more specific than the plurality made them out to be. The plurality's decision flagrantly disregards clear legislative will and an agency's actions thereunder.

▶ ANALYSIS

As Justice Rehnquist stated, the findings of the Court were "all over the place." In fact, one wonders how the plurality and the dissent could have been talking about the same administrative action. When courts have to delve into areas on the edge of human knowledge, such problems are unavoidable.

■ ═ ■

Johnson v. Robison

Veterans Administration (D) v. Conscientious objector (P)

415 U.S. 361 (1974).

NATURE OF CASE: Action to declare a veteran's benefits statute unconstitutional.

FACT SUMMARY: Robison (P) sought a declaratory judgment that veterans' benefits legislation was unconstitutional, but the question of statutory preclusion of judicial review arose.

🏛 RULE OF LAW
A statute prohibiting judicial review of decisions by the Administrator of Veterans Affairs does not bar federal courts from deciding the constitutionality of veterans' benefits legislation.

FACTS: A draftee accorded Class I-O conscientious objector status and who completed performance of required alternate civilian service did not qualify under 38 U.S.C. § 1652(a)(1) as a "veteran . . . who served on active duty" (defined in 38 U.S.C. § 101(21) as "full-time duty in the Armed Forces") and was thus not an "eligible vetcran" entitled under 38 U.S.C. § 1661(a) to veterans' educational benefits provided by the Veterans Administration (D) and the Administrator of Veterans Affairs, Johnson (D). Robison (P), who was such a conscientious objector, was therefore denied educational assistance. He commenced a class action suit for a declaratory judgment that the aforementioned statutes, read together, were unconstitutional. Johnson (D) moved to dismiss the action because 38 U.S.C. § 211(a) prohibited judicial review of decisions of the Administrator. The motion was denied and the court found that the statutes violated the Equal Protection Clause.

ISSUE: Does a statute prohibiting judicial review of the Veterans Affairs Administrator's decisions bar federal courts from deciding the constitutionality of veterans' benefits legislation?

HOLDING AND DECISION: (Brennan, J.) No. A statute prohibiting judicial review of decisions by the Administrator does not bar federal courts from deciding the constitutionality of veterans' benefits legislation. As a statute barring judicial review of the constitutionality question would itself raise questions of its constitutionality, this Court will abide by one of its cardinal principles and first ascertain whether a construction is fairly possible by which the constitutional question may be avoided. It is. The statute addresses itself to the nonreviewability of decisions of the Administrator, not to the nonreviewability of statutes. Thus, there is no statutory preclusion of the judicial review Robison (P) seeks.

▶ ANALYSIS

In 1972, there was a challenge to the no-review clause at issue in this case as it applied to the Administrator's decisions. The court held it did not violate due process. Thus, in the absence of constitutional claims, Veterans Administration decisions remain immune from judicial review.

■━■

Quicknotes

38 U.S.C. § 1661 Entitles veterans to certain benefits.

JUDICIAL REVIEW The authority of the courts to review decisions, actions or omissions committed by another agency or branch of government.

38 U.S.C. § 211(a) Prohibits judicial review of certain decisions by Veterans Administrations.

■━■

Webster v. Doe

CIA (D) v. Former employee (P)

486 U.S. 592 (1988).

NATURE OF CASE: Appeal from vacation of denial of claim for reinstatement.

FACT SUMMARY: When the Central Intelligence Agency (CIA) (D) terminated Doe's (P) employment on learning that he was homosexual, Doe (P) filed an action alleging statutory and constitutional violations by Webster (D), the CIA (D) director.

🏛 RULE OF LAW
Under § 102(c) of the National Security Act, employee termination decisions made by the Director of the Central Intelligence Agency are not judicially reviewable.

FACTS: After working for the Central Intelligence Agency (CIA) (D) for nine years and being consistently rated as an excellent or outstanding employee, John Doe's (P) employment was terminated after he revealed to the CIA (D) that he was a homosexual. Webster (D), director of the CIA (D), concluded that Doe's (P) homosexuality presented a security threat. Doe (P) passed a polygraph test concerning possible security violations, denied having sexual relations with any foreign nationals, and maintained that he had not disclosed classified information to any of his sexual partners. When Doe (P) refused the CIA's (D) request for him to resign, Webster (D) "deemed it necessary and advisable in the interests of the United States to terminate his employment." Doe (P) then filed an action against Webster (D), who moved for dismissal on the ground that § 102(c) of the National Security Act (NSA) precluded judicial review of his termination decisions. The district court granted Doe's (P) motion for partial summary judgment, determined that the Administrative Procedure Act (APA) provided judicial review of Webster's (D) termination decisions, and found that Doe (P) had been unlawfully discharged because the CIA (D) had not followed the procedures described in its own regulations. The court declined to consider the constitutional claims and ordered Doe (P) reinstated to administrative leave status. The court of appeals vacated the district court's judgment and remanded the case for further proceedings, deciding first that judicial review of the CIA's (D) decision was not precluded and that the CIA (D) regulations cited by Doe (P) did not limit Webster's (D) discretion in making termination decisions.

ISSUE: Under § 102(c) of the NSA, are employee termination decisions made by the Director of the CIA judicially reviewable?

HOLDING AND DECISION: (Rehnquist, C.J.) No. Under § 102(c) of the NSA, employee termination decisions made by the Director of the CIA are not judicially

reviewable. Section 701(a) of the APA limits application of the entire APA to situations in which judicial review is not precluded by statute; subsection (a)(1) is concerned with whether Congress expressed an intent to prohibit judicial review, while subsection (a)(2) applies "in those rare instances where 'statutes are drawn in such broad terms that in a given case there is no law to apply.'" The standard set in § 102(c) of the NSA defers to the director and appears to foreclose the application of any meaningful judicial standard of review. Thus, the language and structure of § 102(c) indicate that Congress meant to commit individual employee discharges to the director's discretion and that § 701(a)(2) accordingly precludes judicial review of these decisions under the APA. However, nothing in § 102(c) demonstrates that Congress meant to preclude consideration of colorable constitutional claims arising out of the actions of the director pursuant to that section. Reversed [as to judicial review of terminations under § 102(c)]; remanded [for consideration of Doe's (P) constitutional claims].

CONCURRENCE AND DISSENT: (O'Connor, J.) Because § 102(c) does not provide a meaningful standard for judicial review, such decisions are clearly "committed to agency discretion by law" within the meaning of § 702(a)(2) of the APA. However, the Court erroneously concludes that a constitutional claim challenging the validity of an employment decision covered by § 102(c) may nonetheless be brought in a federal district court. Congress has the power to close the lower federal courts to constitutional claims in this context, and § 102(c) plainly indicates that Congress has done exactly that. The Court points to nothing in the structure, purpose, or legislative history of the NSA that would suggest a different conclusion.

DISSENT: (Scalia, J.) Congress can prescribe, at least within broad limits, that for certain jobs the dismissal decision will be unreviewable—that is, will be "committed to agency discretion by law." Further, it is entirely beyond doubt that if Congress intended to exclude judicial review of the President's decision (through the Director of Central Intelligence) to dismiss an officer of the CIA (D), that disposition would be constitutionally permissible.

▶ ANALYSIS

On remand, *Doe v. Webster*, 769 F. Supp. 1 (D.D.C. 1991), the district court concluded that CIA (D) regulations gave Doe (P) a postprobation property interest in his position and that his discharge without a statement of reasons why his homosexuality posed a security threat and an opportunity to

Continued on next page.

respond to those reasons violated due process. Contrary to the opinion expressed by both Justices O'Connor and Scalia that judicial review of constitutional claims is also precluded in this context, the majority's rejection of all arguments made on this point by Webster (D) sends a clear message that a legislative attempt to preclude review of constitutional claims would be unacceptable. Further, even where national security is concerned, methods exist to balance the need of the individual asserting constitutional claims against the extraordinary needs of the CIA (D) for confidentiality.

■≡■

Quicknotes

NSA § 102   Precludes judicial review of CIA's employment decisions.

APA, § 701   Makes administrative decisions subject to judicial review.

APA § 706   Does not allow arbitrary and capricious agency decisions.

■≡■

Dunlop v. Bachowski

Department of Labor (D) v. Union candidate (P)

421 U.S. 560 (1975).

NATURE OF CASE: Appeal of reversal of dismissal of action to set aside a union election.

FACT SUMMARY: The Department of Labor (D) refused, without explanation, to set aside a labor union election.

🏛 RULE OF LAW
Judicial review of a Department of Labor decision not to overturn a union election is limited to an assessment of whether the decision was arbitrary and capricious.

FACTS: Bachowski (P) lost an election for district director of the United Steelworkers of America (D) by a scant margin. Bachowski (P) protested to the Department of Labor (D) that voting irregularities had occurred. Following an investigation, the Department of Labor (D) refused, without explanation, to take action. Bachowski (P) brought an action to compel the Department of Labor (D) to set aside the election. The district court dismissed, holding that judicial review of such decisions did not exist. The court of appeals reversed, holding that full review of the soundness of such a decision did exist.

ISSUE: Is judicial review of a Department of Labor decision not to overturn a union election limited to an assessment of whether the decision was arbitrary and capricious?

HOLDING AND DECISION: (Brennan, J.) Yes. Judicial review of a Department of Labor (D) decision not to overturn a union election is limited to an assessment of whether the decision was arbitrary and capricious. The statute involved relies upon the special knowledge and discretion of the Department of Labor (D) in deciding whether or not to file suit. Therefore, although this Court does not infer from this that the Department of Labor (D) is immune from suit, the Court will not allow a lower court to substitute its judgment for that of the Department (D). Only when it is shown that the decision is arbitrary will such judgment be overturned. In this instance, such a determination must be made by the district court. Reversed.

CONCURRENCE: (Burger, C.J.) It must be emphasized that the scope of review is exceedingly narrow.

CONCURRENCE AND DISSENT: (Rehnquist, J.) The Department of Labor (D) action should be free from judicial review.

▶ ANALYSIS

The Court required the Department of Labor (D) to provide a detailed explanation for its action or inaction. Such explanations are required of agencies under many statutes. In the absence of such documentation, judicial review is quite difficult.

■■■■

Quicknotes

ARBITRARY AND CAPRICIOUS STANDARD Standard imposed in reviewing the decision of an agency or court when the decision may have been made in disregard of the facts or law.

JUDICIAL REVIEW The authority of the courts to review decisions, actions, or omissions committed by another agency or branch of government.

29 U.S.C. § 452 Requires Labor Secretary to investigate union election complaints.

■■■■

Heckler v. Chaney

Food and Drug Administration (D) v. Death row prisoner (P)

470 U.S. 821 (1985).

NATURE OF CASE: Appeal of reversal of dismissal of action to compel Food and Drug Administration enforcement proceedings.

FACT SUMMARY: Chaney (P) brought an action to compel the Food and Drug Administration (D) to stop the use of lethal drugs in executions.

🏛 RULE OF LAW
A decision by the FDA to refrain from enforcement proceedings is not subject to judicial review.

FACTS: The Food, Drug, and Cosmetic Act mandated that the Food and Drug Administration (FDA) (D) take steps to prevent unauthorized or dangerous uses of approved drugs. Chaney (P), contending that use of approved drugs for execution by injection constituted an unauthorized and dangerous use of drugs, petitioned the FDA (D) to take steps to prevent such use. The FDA (D) declined. Chaney (P) brought an action to compel the FDA (D) to take such steps. The district court granted the FDA (D) summary judgment and dismissed, holding that such agency actions were unreviewable. The appellate court reversed, holding that such actions were reviewable, and further held the decision by the FDA (D) to be improper.

ISSUE: Is a decision by the FDA to refrain from enforcement proceedings subject to judicial review?

HOLDING AND DECISION: (Rehnquist, J.) No. A decision by the FDA (D) to refrain from enforcement proceedings is not subject to judicial review. Traditionally, agency decisions to decline enforcement proceedings have been unreviewable. This is largely due to a respect for the greater knowledge that an agency will be presumed to have over that of a court. Another reason is that agency lack of enforcement generally does not involve coercive intrusion upon personal liberty, the protection of which is the main concern of the courts. As the Act in question gives no hint of an exception of this rule, the decision of the court of appeals must be reversed.

CONCURRENCE: (Marshall, J.) Refusals to enforce should be reviewable in the absence of clear and convincing legislative intent to the contrary.

▶ *ANALYSIS*

Judicial unreviewability of agency inaction is often likened to prosecutorial discretion. In both instances, societal, not individual, interests are at stake. Justice Marshall takes issue with the analogy, contending that societal interests in criminal prosecutions are much more intangible than agency decisions.

■══■

Quicknotes

APA, § 701 Makes administrative decisions subject to judicial review.

FOOD, DRUG, AND COSMETIC ACT Requires the FDA to approve drugs as safe and effective before distribution is allowed.

JUDICIAL REVIEW The authority of the courts to review decisions, actions, or omissions committed by another agency or branch of government.

■══■

Massachusetts v. Environmental Protection Agency

States (P) v. Federal agency (D)

549 U.S. 497 (2007).

NATURE OF CASE: Appeal from federal appeals court ruling.

FACT SUMMARY: Massachusetts (P) and several other states petitioned the Environmental Protection Agency (EPA) (D), asking the EPA (D) to regulate emissions of carbon dioxide and other gases from new motor vehicles, which allegedly contribute to global warming. The EPA (D) denied the petition, claiming that the Clean Air Act does not authorize the agency (D) to regulate greenhouse gas emissions and that even if it were so authorized, the agency (D) had discretion to defer a decision.

🏛 RULE OF LAW

(1) The Clean Air Act gives the Environmental Protection Agency (D) authority to regulate carbon dioxide and other greenhouse gases.

(2) The Environmental Protection Agency (D) may not decline to issue emission standards for motor vehicles based on policy considerations not enumerated in the Clean Air Act.

FACTS: Massachusetts (P) and several other states petitioned the Environmental Protection Agency (EPA) (D), asking the EPA (D) to regulate emissions of carbon dioxide and other gases from new motor vehicles, which allegedly contribute to global warming. Massachusetts (P) argued that the EPA (D) was required to regulate these greenhouse gases by the Clean Air Act, which provides that Congress must regulate "any air pollutant" that may "reasonably be anticipated to endanger public health or welfare." The EPA (D) denied the petition, claiming that the Clean Air Act does not authorize the agency (D) to regulate greenhouse gas emissions. The EPA (D) argued that even if it were so authorized, the agency (D) had discretion to defer a decision until more research could be done on "the causes, extent and significance of climate change and the potential options for addressing it." Massachusetts (P) appealed the denial of the petition to the Court of Appeals for the D.C. Circuit, and a divided panel ruled in favor of the EPA (D).

ISSUE:

(1) Does the Clean Air Act give the EPA authority to regulate carbon dioxide and other greenhouse gases?

(2) May the EPA decline to issue emission standards for motor vehicles based on policy considerations not enumerated in the Clean Air Act?

HOLDING AND DECISION: (Stevens, J.)

(1) Yes. The Clean Air Act gives the EPA (D) authority to regulate carbon dioxide and other greenhouse gases. The EPA's (D) argument that the Clean Air Act was not meant to refer to carbon emissions in the section giving the EPA authority to regulate air pollution agents is without merit. The Act's definition of air pollutant was written with sweeping, broad language so that it would not become obsolete. Its definition of "air pollutant" includes any air pollution agency, including any physical, chemical substance or matter that enters the ambient air. Carbon dioxide, methane, nitrous oxide, and hydrofluorocarbons, which emit from motor vehicles, are without doubt physical and chemical substances that are emitted into the ambient air. The statute unambiguously contemplates greenhouse gases from new motor vehicles, and EPA (D) has authority to regulate emission of those gases.

(2) No. The EPA (D) may not decline to issue emission standards for motor vehicles based on policy considerations not enumerated in the Clean Air Act. The EPA (D) was unjustified in delaying its decision on the basis of prudential and policy considerations. If the EPA (D) wishes to continue its inaction on carbon regulation, it is required by the Act to base the decision on a consideration of whether greenhouse gas emissions contribute to climate change. If it cannot, it has a statutory obligation to act. Reversed and remanded.

DISSENT: (Scalia, J.) The Clean Air Act was intended to combat conventional lower-atmosphere pollutants and not global climate change. It does not require the EPA (D) to make a judgment whenever a petition for rulemaking is filed. Congress knows how to make private action force an agency's hand, and if it wanted to do so here, it would have. Even assuming the EPA's (D) discretion is not unbounded, and assuming that, without reasonable basis for deferring judgment, it must act, the majority is wrong to reject all of the EPA's (D) judgments without basis in text or precedent.

▶ *ANALYSIS*

Massachusetts v. EPA is an historic opinion, in that the Supreme Court stopped just short of ordering the federal government to actively participate in limiting carbon emissions most responsible for global warming. Through its holding, the Court tried to ensure that agencies actually exercise expert judgment free from outside political pressures, especially political pressures emanating from the White House or political appointees in the agencies.

■≡■

Norton v. Southern Utah Wilderness Alliance

Secretary of Interior (D) v. Environmental group (P)

542 U.S. 55 (2004).

NATURE OF CASE: Suit for declaratory and injunctive relief challenging federal management of potential wilderness areas.

FACT SUMMARY: The Bureau of Land Management (BLM) (D) permitted the use of off-road vehicles on federal lands in Utah. The Southern Utah Wilderness Alliance (P) sued the BLM (D) and others for an alleged failure to satisfy the BLM's (D) statutory mandate to manage such lands in a way that did not impair their suitability as wilderness.

RULE OF LAW
The Administrative Procedure Act, 5 U.S.C. § 706(1), does not provide a right of action for an agency's failure to take a general action that it is not required to take.

FACTS: The Bureau of Land Management (BLM) (D) permitted users of potential wilderness areas on federal lands in Utah to operate off-road vehicles (ORVs) for recreational purposes on those lands. ORVs cause significant damage to the lands themselves, to wildlife, and to wilderness enthusiasts. To try to stop such detrimental impacts, the Southern Utah Wilderness Alliance (SUWA) (P) filed suit against the BLM (D) and others, requesting declaratory and injunctive relief requiring the BLM (D) to take action, by changing its management of the use of ORVs, in order to manage its Wilderness Study Areas in Utah "in a manner so as not to impair the suitability of such areas for preservation as wilderness." 43 U.S.C. § 1782(c). [The district court ordered dismissal on the claim challenging the BLM's (D) alleged failure to act, and the court of appeals reversed.] The BLM (D) petitioned the Supreme Court for further review.

ISSUE: Does the Administrative Procedure Act, 5 U.S.C. § 706(1), provide a right of action for an agency's failure to take a general action that it is not required to take?

HOLDING AND DECISION: (Scalia, J.) No. The Administrative Procedure Act (APA) 5 U.S.C. § 706(1), does not provide a right of action for an agency's failure to take a general action that it is not required to take. Sections 702, 704, and 706(1) of the APA all require an "agency action" as the basis for suit, and the APA defines these litigable "agency actions" as discrete actions, not as general, amorphous goals or directives. Even where the APA permits suit for failures to act, the failures must be failures to take "agency actions," which are, by statute, necessarily discrete actions. Moreover, § 706(1) permits suit to compel agency action only when the action is required. Accordingly, there is no right of action even as against discrete agency action if the agency action is

not required by law. The basis of the SUWA's (P) claim against the BLM (D), 42 U.S.C. § 1782(c), does mandate a goal for the BLM (D), but it also grants a broad discretion to the BLM (D) for deciding how to achieve the mandated goal. The total exclusion of ORVs, for example, certainly is not mandated by the non-impairment statute—at any rate, not with the clarity required by Section 706(1). These limitations imposed by the APA serve the legislative purpose, as they do in this case, of prohibiting the courts from interfering with the discretion vested in administrative agencies. Reversed and remanded.

ANALYSIS

Principles of separation of powers and judicial restraint pervade administrative law. Here the Court defers to congressional requirements for reviewability, as established by 5 U.S.C. § 706(1), and the Administrative Procedure Act itself in turn exists largely to protect executive-branch agencies from what Justice Scalia calls "undue judicial interference with their lawful discretion." The Court was unanimous in *Southern Utah Wilderness Alliance*, which demonstrates how clearly those fundamental principles apply in this case.

Quicknotes

INJUNCTIVE RELIEF A court order issued as a remedy, requiring a person to do, or prohibiting that person from doing, a specific act.

JUDICIAL RESTRAINT Self-imposed discipline by judges making decisions without indulging their own personal views or ideas that may not be consistent with existing law.

Dalton v. Specter

Parties not identified.

511 U.S. 462 (1994).

NATURE OF CASE: Appeal from holding that judicial review of administrative action was permissible.

FACT SUMMARY: A coalition of employees and state officials (P) sought to enjoin the Secretary of Defense (D) from closing the Philadelphia Naval Shipyard.

🏛 RULE OF LAW
Judicial review of administrative decisions is limited to final agency actions that directly affect the litigant.

FACTS: Pursuant to the Defense Base Closure and Realignment Act of 1990, the President authorized closure of the Philadelphia Naval Shipyard. Under the Act, after a public notice and comment period, the Secretary of Defense (D) prepared a closure and realignment list based upon certain criteria. This list was submitted to Congress and to the Defense Base Closure and Realignment Commission (D). The Commission (D) then held public hearings and prepared a report containing an assessment of the Secretary's (D) recommendations and the Commission's (D) own recommendations for base closures and realignments. The President then decided whether to approve or disapprove of the closures. The decision to close the Philadelphia Naval shipyard resulted from this process. However, before the President could submit his certification of approval to Congress, the coalition (P) filed suit. The suit claimed that Secretaries of Defense and Navy (D) had violated substantive and procedural requirements of the 1990 Act, and the Commission's (D) recommendation process had used improper selection criteria. The court of appeals held that judicial review of the decision was available to ensure that the various participants in the selection process had complied with the procedural mandates specified by Congress. The Supreme Court granted review, vacated the judgment, and remanded for further consideration. The court of appeals adhered to its first decision, and the Secretary of Defense (D) sought review.

ISSUE: Is judicial review of administrative decisions limited to final agency actions that directly affect the litigant?

HOLDING AND DECISION: (Rehnquist, C.J.) Yes. Judicial review of administrative decisions is limited to final agency actions that directly affect the litigant. The prerequisite to review under the Administrative Procedure Act (APA) depends upon whether the agency action is final. Finality is determined by whether the agency has completed its decision-making process and whether the result of that process is one that will directly affect the parties. Here, the reports submitted by the Secretary of Defense (D) and the Commission (D) carry no direct consequences for base closings. It is crucial to recognize that the President, not the Commission (D), takes the final action that affects the military installations. Moreover, the President's actions are not reviewable under the APA, because the President is not an agency within the meaning of the APA. Therefore, the decisions made pursuant to the 1990 Act are not reviewable under the APA. Reversed.

CONCURRENCE: (Souter, J.) It is unnecessary to reach the question of whether the Commission (D) report is a final agency action. The text, structure, and purpose of the Base Closure Act compel the conclusion that judicial review of the Commission's (D) or the Secretary's (D) actions under the Act is precluded. The Act grants the President unfettered discretion to accept or reject the Commission's (D) report.

▶ ANALYSIS

Each of the opinions issued in this case made note of Congress's detailed legislative scheme. While the majority held review unavailable on grounds of standing, the concurring justices stated that the unusual legislative scheme precluded judicial review of decisions thereunder. Each decision effectively states that judicial review is inappropriate where congressional action has permissibly foreclosed it.

■══■

Quicknotes

ADMINISTRATIVE PROCEDURE ACT (APA) Enacted in 1946 to govern practices and proceedings before federal administrative agencies.

JUDICIAL REVIEW The authority of the courts to review decisions, actions, or omissions committed by another agency or branch of government.

■══■

Abbott Laboratories v. Gardner

Drug manufacturer (P) v. Department of Health, Education, and Welfare (D)

387 U.S. 136 (1967).

NATURE OF CASE: Appeal of reversal of summary judgment in challenge to certain agency regulations.

FACT SUMMARY: The Department of Health, Education, and Welfare (D) promulgated regulations concerning how drugs could be labeled when promoted and marketed.

🏛 RULE OF LAW
A district court has jurisdiction to consider a preenforcement challenge to regulations concerning drug labeling.

FACTS: Acting under amendments to the federal Food, Drug and Cosmetic Act, the Department of Health, Education, and Welfare (D) promulgated regulations mandating that drug manufacturers had to display the "established" (generic) name of drugs promoted or marketed along with the trade name in every instance in which the trade name was used. Various drug manufacturers sued for injunctive and declaratory relief, contending that the regulation exceeded statutory authority. The district court granted Abbott Laboratories' (P) and the other plaintiffs' motion for summary judgment on this issue, but the court of appeals reversed, holding that preenforcement review of the regulations was unavailable.

ISSUE: Does a district court have jurisdiction to consider a preenforcement challenge to regulations concerning drug labeling?

HOLDING AND DECISION: (Harlan, J.) Yes. A district court has jurisdiction to consider a preenforcement challenge to regulations concerning drug labeling. The presumption is that administrative action is reviewable, so unless something in the statute in question or the Administrative Procedure Act bars review, it is available. The Federal Food, Drug, and Cosmetic Act contains several provisions enumerating review procedures, but nothing in the statute suggests these are to be exclusive, and, in fact, the Act states they shall not be exclusive. Secondly, the regulations are "final agency actions" within the meaning of the Administrative Procedure Act. Once regulations have been promulgated, agency rulemaking action is final. A concerned party need not wait for enforcement efforts to challenge the regulations. Reversed.

▶ ANALYSIS

The Government (D) made a ripeness argument. It contended that review was only available during enforcement proceedings. The Court was of the opinion that the end of the rulemaking process was a better time to consider agency action final because the issues could be resolved before time and effort were spent on attempted enforcement of possibly invalid regulations.

■■■

Quicknotes

APA, § 702 Allows for judicial review of agency action by adversely affected parties.

FOOD, DRUG, AND COSMETIC ACT Amended in 1962 to require prescription drugs to be labeled with generic name.

RIPENESS A doctrine precluding a federal court from hearing or determining a matter unless it constitutes an actual and present controversy warranting a determination by the court.

■■■

Toilet Goods Association v. Gardner

Business (P) v. FDA (D)

387 U.S. 158 (1967).

NATURE OF CASE: Action to enjoin enforcement of an administrative regulation.

FACT SUMMARY: Pursuant to a statutory mandate to "promulgate regulations for the efficient enforcement" of the Food and Drug Act, the Food and Drug Administration (FDA) commissioner (D) formulated a regulation that provided for the suspension of any company that refused the FDA (D) access to its facilities.

🏛 RULE OF LAW
The test for determining whether a federal administrative regulation is ripe for review is not satisfied where (1) there is not a concrete context of specific enforcement procedures and (2) no hardship will inure to an aggrieved party from being forced to await delayed review.

FACTS: Congress, by statute, empowered the Food and Drug Administration (FDA) commissioner (D) to "promulgate regulations for the efficient enforcement" of the Food and Drug Act. Pursuant to this power, the commissioner promulgated a regulation giving itself the power to suspend the federal certification service for any company which refused access to its facilities to FDA (D) inspectors and employees. Because Congress had repeatedly denied the FDA (D) this very sanction that the FDA now granted to itself, Toilet Goods Association (P) filed this action for an injunction against enforcement of the regulation and a declaratory judgment that it was an illegal extension of FDA (D) power. After the court of appeals held that the action should be dismissed as not ripe for judicial determination, this appeal followed.

ISSUE: Should a court ordinarily wait until a concrete context of specific enforcement procedures has been promulgated before reviewing a discretionary administrative agency regulation where no hardship will inure to the aggrieved party because of such delay?

HOLDING AND DECISION: (Harlan, J.) Yes. The test for determining whether a federal administration regulation is ripe for judicial review is not satisfied where (1) there isn't a concrete context of specific enforcement procedures and (2) no hardship will inure to an aggrieved party from being forced to await a delayed review. Neither part of the test is satisfied here. The regulation which the commissioner promulgated is filled with the word "may," granting him wide discretion which he "may" use legally or "may" not. Until a set of enforcement procedures are adopted from which the court can determine whether the commissioner will act legally or illegally, review is inappropriate.

Furthermore, Toilet Goods Association (P) has failed to allege any hardship arising from the regulation itself or which might arise from being forced to await review. Toilet Goods Association (P) is not forced to undertake any expense to comply with the commissioner's regulation, and, if they decide to refuse compliance, the suspension they will be handed is subject to speedy administrative and judicial review. Affirmed.

CONCURRENCE: (Fortas, J.) Established principles of jurisprudence, solidly rooted in the constitutional structure of our government, require that the courts should not intervene in the administrative process in a shotgun fashion. Where Congress has provided a method of review, the requisite showing to induce the courts otherwise to bring a governmental program to a halt may not be made by a mere showing of the impact of the regulation and the customary hardships of interim compliance. Courts cannot properly—and should not—attempt to judge in the abstract and generally whether a regulation is within the statutory scheme.

▶ ANALYSIS

Toilet Goods, a companion case of *Abbott Laboratories*, 387 U.S. 136 (1967), defined the outer limits of the new, broadened "ripeness" standard which the latter established for logical review of administrative regulations. Note that, in doing so, *Toilet Goods* reiterates and reinforces the traditional Article III function of the ripeness doctrine—that is, that issues be presented in a concrete context so as to avoid advisory opinions and assure the best jurisprudential determination of the questions involved. It is important, however, to differentiate this case from cases in which final administrative orders and findings, carrying burdensome adverse collateral consequences, are handed down by agencies. Such orders, which, implicitly, at least, decide concrete rights of particular parties, are ripe for judicial review. The leading case on such orders, *Frozen Food Express v. United States*, 351 U.S. 40 (1956), involved an Interstate Commerce Commission (ICC) order declaring certain agricultural commodities (which Frozen Food carried interstate) to be nonexempt from certain ICC regulations. The fact of the necessary adverse collateral consequences for Frozen Food presented the issue of legality within a concrete context—unlike the purely speculative context which *Toilet Goods* anticipated—and made review appropriate.

■=■

Continued on next page.

Quicknotes

FOOD AND DRUG ACT Empowers the agency to promulgate rules regarding color additives.

RIPENESS A doctrine, precluding a federal court from hearing or determining a matter unless it constitutes an actual and present controversy, warranting a determination by the court.

■━■

Association of Data Processing Service Organizations, Inc. v. Camp

Trade group (P) v. Comptroller of the Currency (D)

397 U.S. 150 (1970).

NATURE OF CASE: Suit challenging a ruling of the Comptroller of the Currency.

FACT SUMMARY: The Association of Data Processing Service Organizations, Inc. (Association) (P) challenged a ruling of the Comptroller of the Currency (D) that national banks could perform data processing services for customers and other banks. The Comptroller (D) attacked the Association's (P) standing to prosecute the suit.

🏛 RULE OF LAW
Standing to challenge an order of an administrative agency is established by a showing that the interest sought to be protected is arguably within the zone of interests to be regulated by the statute or the constitutional guarantee in question.

FACTS: The Association of Data Processing Service Organizations, Inc. (Association) (P) challenged a ruling by the Comptroller of the Currency (D) which allowed national banks, as an incident to their banking services, to make their data processing services available to other banks and to bank customers. The district court dismissed the suit, holding that the Association (P) lacked standing to prosecute the action.

ISSUE: May an administrative ruling which pertains to a particular industry be challenged by an outside party whose interests will be adversely affected by that ruling?

HOLDING AND DECISION: (Douglas, J.) Yes. Administrative orders may be challenged by anyone who alleges an injury to an interest which is arguably within the zone of interests intended to be protected or regulated by the statute or the constitutional guarantee in question. Section 4 of the Bank Service Corporation Act prohibits any bank from engaging in the performance of any activity other than that of providing banking services. It is apparent from the legislative history of this enactment that it was intended in part to protect entities which, like the Association (P), would suffer financial or other harm were the banks permitted to engage in nonbanking activities. Accordingly, the Association (P) has standing to prosecute this action.

▶ ANALYSIS

Issues of standing are almost always determined in favor of the party whose right to bring a suit is being challenged. More and more, standing is being accorded plaintiffs whose interests are nonmonetary, indirect, or minimal. Frequently, determination of the standing issue will depend upon the availability of other plaintiffs whose interests in pursuing an

action are more concrete than are those of the party presently before the court. But the fact that a party is not the best of all possible plaintiffs will not alone justify a ruling that he lacks standing to prosecute an action. It is anticipated that the evident judicial tendency to confer standing upon even the more dubious plaintiffs will result in the formulation of ever-more-imaginative bases upon which standing might be predicated.

■==■

Quicknotes

BANK SERVICE ACT, § 4 Prohibits banks from engaging in services other than banking.

STANDING Whether a party possesses the right to commence suit against another party by having a personal stake in the resolution of the controversy.

ZONE OF INTERESTS The range or category of interests that a constitutional guarantee or statute is intended to protect.

■==■

National Credit Union Administration v. First National Bank & Trust Co.

Credit union organization (D) v. Bank (P)

522 U.S. 479 (1998).

NATURE OF CASE: Appeal from a reversal of judgment dismissing complaint challenging agency approval of credit union membership.

FACT SUMMARY: First National Bank & Trust Co. (P) contended that the National Credit Union Administration (D) had impermissibly expanded the membership definitions of federal credit unions.

🏛 RULE OF LAW
Prudential standing is established when the interest sought to be protected by the complainant is arguably within the zone of interests to be protected or regulated by the statute in question.

FACTS: The Federal Credit Union Act (FCUA) provided that federal credit union membership be limited to groups having a common bond of occupation or association, or to groups within a well-defined neighborhood, community, or rural district. Since 1982, however, the National Credit Union Administration (NCUA) (D) had interpreted the FCUA to permit federal credit unions to be composed of unrelated employer groups, wherein each employer group had its own common bond. Once NCUA (D) expanded membership criteria, AT&T Family Credit Union (ATTF) expanded its operations. Upon NCUA (D) approval of ATTF's continued expansion, First National Bank & Trust Co. (First National) (P) and several other banks (P) brought suit under the Administrative Procedure Act (APA). The district court dismissed the complaint, holding that First National (P) et al. lacked standing to challenge the NCUA's (D) decision because their interests did not fall within the "zone of interests" to be protected under the FCUA. The court of appeals reversed and remanded. The district court then determined that NCUA (D) had acted permissibly. The court of appeals again reversed, and the Supreme Court granted certiorari.

ISSUE: Is prudential standing established when the interest sought to be protected by the complainant is arguably within the zone of interests to be protected or regulated by the statute in question?

HOLDING AND DECISION: (Thomas, J.) Yes. Prudential standing is established when the interest sought to be protected by the complainant is arguably within the zone of interests to be protected or regulated by the statute in question. Whether a potentially protected interest falls within the zone of interests of the statute is a two-part test. First, the interests protected by the statute must be discerned. Then, the inquiry focuses on whether the complainant's interests, as affected by the agency action, are among these statutory interests. Here, one of the interests arguably to be protected by the FCUA was an interest in limiting the markets that federal credit unions can serve. As a competitor of federal credit unions, First National (P) has an interest in limiting the markets that federal credit unions can serve. NCUA (D) has affected that interest by allowing federal credit unions to increase their customer base. Affirmed.

DISSENTING: (O'Conner, J.) The majority's analysis is not in concert with previous case law in which a plaintiff has alleged that agency action has caused competitive injury to its commercial interests. In such cases, the focus is on whether competitive injury to the commercial interest falls within the zone of interests protected by the relevant statute. Here, the terms of the FCUA do not suggest a concern with protecting interests of competitors. Instead the statute works to ensure that each credit union remains a cooperative institution that is economically stable and responsive to its members needs.

▶ ANALYSIS

The so-called prudential standing test involving a zone of interest ensures that judicial review does not undermine congressional design of administrative programs by adding to Article III's requirements. Under Article III, a plaintiff must establish standing by proving: (1) injury-in-fact, a direct and personal harm; (2) caused by or fairly traceable to the defendant; and (3) redressable by the remedy sought. The Administrative Procedure Act, basically a codification of the Article III standing requirements, nowhere mentions anything about a "zone of interests." The term "zone of interests" first appeared in *Association of Data Processing Service Organizations, Inc. v. Camp*, 397 U.S. 150 (1970).

■━■

Quicknotes

APA, § 10(a) Provides for a general right of judicial review.

FEDERAL CREDIT UNION ACT, § 109 Limits credit union membership to groups with common bonds of occupation or association.

STANDING Whether a party possesses the right to commence suit against another party by having a personal stake in the resolution of the controversy.

ZONE OF INTERESTS The range or category of interests that a constitutional guarantee or statute is intended to protect.

■━■

Sierra Club v. Morton

Environmental group (P) v. United States Forest Service (D)

405 U.S. 727 (1972).

NATURE OF CASE: Appeal from denial of preliminary injunction to restrain federal officials from granting permits to developer.

FACT SUMMARY: The Sierra Club (P) sued to enjoin federal Forestry and Interior Officials (D) from permitting Walt Disney Enterprises to build a highway in a protected national park area.

🏛 RULE OF LAW
Mere interest in a problem does not in itself render an organization "adversely affected" or "aggrieved" within the meaning of the Administrative Procedure Act.

FACTS: Mineral King Valley is a designated game refuge included within the Sequoia National Forest by special Act of Congress. The United States Forest Service (Service) (D), which maintains and administers the national forests, began considering the Valley for recreational development during the 1940s. Noticing the demand for skiing facilities, the Service (D) invited bids from private developers for the construction and operation of a ski resort that would also serve as a summer recreation area. Walt Disney Enterprises won the bidding. The approved Disney plan involved motels, restaurants, parking lots, and multiple other structures that would accommodate 14,000 visitors daily. The facilities would require additional highways and power line construction that would have to be approved by the Department of the Interior (D). The Sierra Club (P), which favored maintaining the Valley in its present state, filed suit in district court seeking a declaratory judgment invalidating the proposed development, along with preliminary and permanent injunctive relief. The Sierra Club (P) sued as a membership corporation with a special interest in the conservation and maintenance of the national parks and game refuges. The district court granted the preliminary injunction. The Ninth Circuit Court of Appeals reversed for lack of standing. The Sierra Club (P) appealed.

ISSUE: Does the law require more than mere interest in a problem to render an organization "adversely affected" or "aggrieved" within the meaning of the Administrative Procedure Act?

HOLDING AND DECISION: (Stewart, J.) Yes. Mere interest in a problem does not in itself render an organization "adversely affected" or "aggrieved" within the meaning of the Administrative Procedure Act (APA). The injury-in-fact test requires more than injury to a cognizable interest. It requires that the party seeking review be among the injured. Here, the alleged injury would be directly felt by those persons using the Park and Valley for whom the aesthetic and recreational value would be lessened by the proposed construction. Nowhere in its pleadings or affidavits did the Sierra Club (P) allege that it or its members use the Valley for any purpose, much less that their use of the Valley would be significantly affected by the Disney development. Affirmed.

DISSENT: (Douglas, J.) It should be permissible to litigate environmental issues before federal agencies and courts in the name of the inanimate object about to be despoiled. Permitting the court to appoint a representative for an inanimate object would be no different from judicial appointment of guardians, conservators, or counsel for the indigent. Such action would allow existing beneficiaries of America's natural wonders to be heard before priceless pieces of Americana are reduced to rubble.

▶ ANALYSIS

The *Sierra Club* Court makes no distinction between injury to non-economic and economic interests. Aesthetic and environmental interests, like economic interests, should be considered important ingredients of life. Hence, environmental interests are equally deserving of protection.

■=■

Quicknotes

APA § 10(a) Provides for a general right of judicial review.

INJURY IN FACT An injury that gives rise to standing to sue.

STANDING Whether a party possesses the right to commence suit against another party by having a personal stake in the resolution of the controversy.

■=■

Federal Election Commission v. Akins

Regulatory agency (D) v. Voters (P)

524 U.S. 11 (1998).

NATURE OF CASE: Court challenge by voters of Federal Election Commission (D) finding.

FACT SUMMARY: Voters appealed a finding by the Federal Election Commission determining that the American Israel Public Affairs Committee is not a "political committee" for purposes of disclosure as required by the Federal Election Campaign Act.

🏛 RULE OF LAW
Voters have standing to challenge a regulatory decision where Congress, through legislation, intended to protect voters from the kind of injury at issue, and harm in fact exists because the injury is sufficiently widespread and concrete.

FACTS: Voter respondents (P) have views that are frequently in opposition to those of the American Israel Public Affairs Committee (AIPAC). In order to compel disclosure of AIPAC membership, contributions, and campaign expenditures, the voters (P) petitioned the Federal Election Commission (FEC) (D) to regard the AIPAC as a "political committee," requiring it to disclose the necessary information pursuant to the Federal Election Campaign Act (Act). The Act imposes penalties on entities spending in coordination with a political campaign, as a means of stemming voting corruption. The FEC (D) found in favor of the AIPAC on the grounds that the voters (P) had no standing to bring the matter to review since the AIPAC was characterized as primarily a issue-lobbying organization and not a campaign committee. In addition, it was alleged that the voters (P) lacked injury and therefore standing to bring suit. The voters (P) appealed.

ISSUE: Do voters have standing to challenge a regulatory decision where Congress, through legislation, intends to protect voters from the kind of injury at issue, and the injury is sufficiently widespread and concrete?

HOLDING AND DECISION: (Breyer, J.) Yes. Voters have standing to challenge a regulatory decision where Congress, through legislation, intended to protect voters from the kind of injury at issue and, harm in fact exists, because the injury is sufficiently widespread and concrete. "Prudential standing" exists where the injury asserted by the plaintiff falls within a range of interests protected by the applicable legislative statute. Furthermore, constitutional standing in the form of "injury in fact" exists where the asserted harm is shared in equal measure by a large or widespread class of citizens. In this case, the injury suffered by the voters (P) as a group is directly traceable to the FEC's (D) decision, even though the agency (D) may have reached the same result lawfully. As a result, standing is conferred upon the plaintiffs to have their case reviewed. Remanded for further proceedings.

DISSENT: (Scalia, J.) The voters' (P) allegations in the instant case are insufficient to render them "aggrieved" for the purpose of finding injury and standing. Their challenge further asserts, in error, that the injury suffered is the result of the defendant's refusal to place the needed information in the public domain. The requirement of a "case or controversy" is necessary to maintain a meaningful separation between the judicial branch of our government and the executive; therefore, Congress may not legislate to permit any person to manage the executive branch's enforcement of the law.

▶ ANALYSIS

The Court here interpreted the voters' challenge to the FEC's (D) initial ruling in two parts: (1) whether the voters (P) were specifically provided for as a group with regard to the legislation governing redress for the injury alleged; and (2) whether Congress actually had the power to authorize courts to adjudicate over these types of suits. In addition, the court divided the standing analysis into "prudential" and "constitutional" forms of standing, requiring that both be satisfied before a suit could be successfully brought before it.

■==■

Quicknotes

REDRESSABILITY Requirement that in order for a court to hear a case there must be an injury that is redressible or capable of being remedied.

STANDING TO SUE Plaintiff must allege that he has a legally predictable interest at stake in the litigation.

■==■

Lujan v. Defenders of Wildlife

Secretary of the Department of the Interior (D) v. Government group (P)

504 U.S. 555 (1992).

NATURE OF CASE: Appeal from denial of motion for summary judgment based upon standing.

FACT SUMMARY: Defenders of Wildlife (P) challenged the Secretary of the Department of the Interior's (D) rule limiting the Endangered Species Act to actions within the United States or on the high seas.

🏛 RULE OF LAW
Standing requires an actual or imminent injury in fact, fairly traceable to agency action and redressable by the court.

FACTS: The Endangered Species Act (Act) protected endangered species of animals from threats to their continued existence. The Act required the Secretary of the Department of the Interior (Secretary) (D) to promulgate a list of endangered species and to define the critical habitat of these species. Each federal agency was then required to work with the Secretary (D) to ensure that any action authorized, funded, or carried out by the agency was not likely to jeopardize the endangered animal or its habitat. The Fish and Wildlife Service and the National Marine Fisheries Service promulgated a regulation that extended the statutory requirements to actions in foreign nations. However, the Department of the Interior (D) limited such actions to those within the United States or on the high seas. Defenders of Wildlife (P) filed suit seeking declaratory judgment that the Secretary's (D) action was contrary to the federal law and requesting injunctive relief requiring the restoration of the initial interpretation. The district court granted the Secretary's (D) motion for summary judgment for lack of standing. The court of appeals reversed, and the Supreme Court granted review.

ISSUE: Does standing require an actual or imminent injury in fact, fairly traceable to agency action and redressable by the court?

HOLDING AND DECISION: (Scalia, J.) Yes. Standing requires an actual or imminent injury in fact, fairly traceable to agency action and redressable by the court. To survive the motion for summary judgment, Defenders of Wildlife (DOW) (P) must establish through specific facts, not only that the listed species were in fact threatened by funded activities abroad, but also that a DOW (P) member would be directly affected by damage to the species. Assuming DOW's (P) affidavits establish threat to one the listed species, the group cannot show that damage to the species will produce imminent harm to any DOW (P) member. Nor does DOW's (P) ecosystem nexus argument work. Any person using a contiguous ecosystem adversely affected by

an activity does not have an injury in fact, unless the person uses the area directly affected by the activity. Nor can the injury-in-fact requirement be satisfied by congressional conferral upon all persons the right to have executive agencies, observe the procedures required by law. Individual rights do not mean public rights that have been legislatively pronounced to belong to each individual who is a member of the public. Reversed.

CONCURRENCE: (Kennedy, J.) On the record, DOW (P) has failed to demonstrate that the group or its members are among the injured. However, the Court should not foreclose the possible that under different circumstances a nexus theory could support a claim of standing. Moreover, Congress may define injuries and articulate chains of causation that will give rise to a case or controversy where none existed previously.

DISSENT: (Blackmun, J.) To survive a motion for summary judgment on standing, DOW's members (P) need not prove that they are actually or imminently harmed. Procedurally, DOW (P) need only show that a genuine issue of material fact exists as to standing. The majority fails to mention the genuine-issue-of-fact standard, instead referring to DOW's (P) presumed failure to provide evidence of injury. Examining the facts contained within the affidavits, it is at least questionable that members of DOW (P) have shown that they would personally suffer imminent harm. Moreover, the majority erroneously questions congressional authority to impose procedural constraints on executive power. Surely the federal courts must enforce administrative procedures when citizen suits authorize such conduct.

▶ ANALYSIS

Lujan appears to deny that Congress can create an injury in fact for which a member of the public can seek judicial review. In essence, *Lujan* seemingly prevents Congress from authorizing private attorneys general to enforce the law. However, a subsequent case, *Bennett v. Spear*, 520 U.S. 154 (1997) reaffirmed the use of generally authorized citizen law suits.

■══■

Quicknotes

ENDANGERED SPECIES ACT, § 7 Requires that all agencies ensure that actions don't endanger certain species.

STANDING Whether a party possesses the right to commence suit against another party by having a personal stake in the resolution of the controversy.

■══■

Massachusetts v. Environmental Protection Agency

States (P) v. Federal agency (D)

549 U.S. 497 (2007).

NATURE OF CASE: Appeal from federal appeals court ruling.

FACT SUMMARY: Massachusetts (P) and several other states petitioned the Environmental Protection Agency (EPA) (D), asking EPA (D) to regulate emissions of carbon dioxide and other gases from new motor vehicles, which allegedly contribute to global warming. EPA (D) denied the petition, claiming that the Clean Air Act does not authorize the agency (D) to regulate greenhouse gas emissions and that even if it were so authorized, the agency (D) had discretion to defer a decision.

RULE OF LAW
States and environmental organizations have standing to sue a government agency for failure to promulgate new motor vehicle greenhouse gas emission standards.

FACTS: Massachusetts (P) and several other states petitioned the Environmental Protection Agency (EPA) (D), asking EPA (D) to regulate emissions of carbon dioxide and other gases from new motor vehicles, which allegedly contribute to global warming. Massachusetts (P) argued that EPA (D) was required to regulate these greenhouse gases by the Clean Air Act, which provides that Congress must regulate "any air pollutant" that may "reasonably be anticipated to endanger public health or welfare." EPA (D) denied the petition, claiming that the Clean Air Act does not authorize the agency (D) to regulate greenhouse gas emissions. EPA (D) argued that even if it were so authorized, the agency (D) had discretion to defer a decision until more research could be done on "the causes, extent and significance of climate change and the potential options for addressing it." Massachusetts (P) appealed the denial of the petition to the Court of Appeals for the D.C. Circuit, and a divided panel ruled in favor of EPA (D).

ISSUE: Do states and environmental organizations have standing to sue a government agency for failure to promulgate new motor vehicle greenhouse gas emission standards?

HOLDING AND DECISION: (Stevens, J.) Yes. States and environmental organizations have standing to sue a government agency for failure to promulgate new motor vehicle greenhouse gas emission standards. Only one of the petitioners needs to have standing in order for the court to consider the petition for review, and Massachusetts (P) does. States are not normal litigants for purposes of standing analysis, and are entitled to special solicitude in standing analysis. The rise in sea levels associated with global warming has already harmed and will continue to harm Massachusetts (P), and such injury associated with climate change is serious and well recognized, even by the EPA (D). In addition, EPA (D) does not dispute the existence of a causal connection between man-made greenhouse gas emissions and global warming. EPA's (D) refusal to regulate greenhouse gas emissions presents a risk of harm to Massachusetts (P) that is both "actual" and "imminent," and there is a "substantial likelihood that the judicial relief requested" will prompt EPA (D) to take steps to reduce that injury. At a minimum, EPA's (D) refusal to regulate such emissions contributes to Massachusetts' (P) injuries. While regulating motor-vehicle emissions will not reverse global warming, it does not follow that the court lacks jurisdiction to decide whether EPA (D) has a duty to take steps to slow or reduce it.

DISSENT: (Roberts, J.) The petitioners in this case bear the burden of alleging an injury that is fairly traceable to the EPA's (D) failure to promulgate new motor vehicle greenhouse gas emission standards, and that is likely to be redressed by the issuance of such standards. The petitioners would have failed to meet its burden, if the majority had not relaxed the standing requirements because the injuries were to a state, instead of a person, without basis in the court's jurisprudence, and without finding support for "special solicitude" in the majority opinion. Even so, the status of Massachusetts (P) as a state cannot compensate for the petitioners' failure to show injury in fact, causation, and redressability. The majority found injury in fact in Massachusetts' (P) loss of coastal land, but the rest of the standing analysis veers away from that particular injury. The concept of global warming seems inconsistent with the particularization requirement of standing analysis—that the alleged injury is "concrete and particularized," and "distinct and palpable." And by finding that if the EPA (D) changes course, the trend affecting Massachusetts' (P) coast will reverse ignores the complexities of global warming. The causation and redressability requirements are also, therefore, not met.

ANALYSIS

Standing was the issue on which the lawsuit appeared most vulnerable, because in recent years the Supreme Court has steadily raised the barrier to standing, especially in environmental cases. But Justice Stevens changed the rules by finding that Massachusetts (P) was due special deference in its claim to standing because of its status as a sovereign state. This is an important alteration in the court's jurisprudence.

■══■

Quicknotes

STANDING The right to commence suit against another party because of a personal stake in the resolution of the controversy.

■══■

Friends of the Earth, Inc. v. Laidlaw Environmental Services

Waste company (D) v. Citizens' group (P)

528 U.S. 167 (2000).

NATURE OF CASE: Appeal of judgment in an action under the Clean Water Act.

FACT SUMMARY: Laidlaw Environmental Services, Inc. (D) operated a hazardous waste incinerator that was discharging mercury into a river at a level high enough to violate its permit, which specified the amount of waste the company could put into the environment. Friends of the Earth, Inc. (P) sued them under the citizen-suit provision of the Act.

> **🏛 RULE OF LAW**
> The plaintiff had standing to sue the defendant for injunctive relief and civil penalties because the plaintiff proved, first, injury in fact, and, second, that penalties would be a deterrent.

FACTS: Laidlaw Environmental Services, Inc. (Laidlaw) (D) operated a hazardous waste incinerator and was granted a permit by the South Carolina Department of Health and Environmental Control, authorizing it to discharge treated water into a river. The permit stated limits on the discharge of pollutants into the river and regulated the flow, temperature, toxicity, and pH of the effluent from the facility; it also imposed monitoring and reporting obligations. Laidlaw's (D) discharges repeatedly exceeded the limits set by the permit. Under the Clean Water Act (Act), Friends of the Earth, Inc. (Friends) (P) filed an action against Laidlaw (D) alleging noncompliance with the permit and seeking injunctive relief and/or civil penalties. The citizen-suit provision of the Act allows people who have an interest and who may or may not be adversely affected in a matter to sue regarding that matter. The district court assessed a civil penalty of $405,800. Laidlaw (D) appealed.

ISSUE: Does Friends (P) have standing to seek both injunctive and civil penalties under the Act?

HOLDING AND DECISION: (Ginsburg, J.) Yes. Friends (P), has standing to seek both injunctive and civil penalties under the Act. Friends (P) had standing to seek injunctive relief because it showed injury in fact by stating that members of Friends (P) were unable to fish, wade, picnic, or participate in other recreational activities in and along the river because it looked and smelled polluted. These statements prove injury in fact because those making them aver that they use the affected area and that, for them, the aesthetic and recreational values of the area are lessened by the challenged activity. Furthermore, Friends (P) had standing to seek civil penalties because all civil penalties have some deterrent effect and, therefore, affords redress to citizen plaintiffs who are injured or threatened with injury as a consequence of ongoing conduct. Moreover, a threat of civil penalties has no deterrent value unless it is credible that it will be carried out; it is reasonable for Congress to conclude that an actual award of penalties does bring deterrence above and beyond the mere prospect of penalties. Affirmed.

DISSENT: (Scalia, J.) Friends (P) did not demonstrate injury in fact. Concern that water was polluted and a belief that the pollution had reduced the value of their homes does not show that they have suffered a concrete and particularized injury. In addition, in regards to redressability, the remedy Friends (P) seeks is inconsistent and doesn't satisfy their allegations of injury. Furthermore, it is unlikely that future polluters will be deterred.

▶ ANALYSIS

In contrast to *Lujan v. National Wildlife Federation*, 497 U.S. 871 (1990), the affidavits in this case assert that Laidlaw's (D) discharges directly affected those affiant's recreational, aesthetic, and economic interests; in *Lujan*, the affidavits merely contained general averments and conclusory allegations. Furthermore, unlike the court in *Steel Company v. Citizens for a Better Environment*, 523 U.S. 83 (1998), which held that citizens lacked standing to seek civil penalties for violations that had abated by the time of the suit because the complaint did not allege any continuing or imminent violation and thus provided no basis for such an allegation, here the court did not reach the issue of standing to seek penalties for violations that are ongoing at the time of the complaint and that could continue in the future.

■=■

Quicknotes

INJURY IN FACT An injury that gives rise to standing to sue.

■=■

CHAPTER 8

Damage Actions Against the Federal Government and Its Officers

Quick Reference Rules of Law

United States v. Mitchell

Federal government (D) v. Native American (P)

463 U.S. 206 (1983).

NATURE OF CASE: Appeal of determination of jurisdiction in action for breach of fiduciary duty.

FACT SUMMARY: Suit was brought against the United States (D) for alleged mismanagement of Indian lands under treaty between the United States (D) and the Quinault Tribe.

🏛 RULE OF LAW
The federal government may be liable for breaches of trust in its management of lands on reservations.

FACTS: By treaty, the Quinault Indian tribe ceded certain lands to the United States (D). Certain lands were reserved for the Indians. The Department of the Interior was to manage the timber resources on the lands for the benefit of the Indians. Mitchell (P) and several other Indians brought an action in the Court of Claims against the United States (D) for alleged mismanagement of the lands. The Court held that jurisdiction existed, and the United States (D) appealed this determination.

ISSUE: May the federal government be liable for breaches of trust in its management of lands on reservations?

HOLDING AND DECISION: (Marshall, J.) Yes. The federal government may be liable for breaches of trust in its management of lands on reservations. The Tucker Act (Act) constitutes a waiver of sovereign immunity but does not create any enforceable rights. However, the Act under which lands were ceded to the Indians places the Government (D) in a fiduciary relationship with the Indians in its management of the Indian lands. An action for breach of fiduciary duties is therefore possible, as is the case with any fiduciary. Affirmed.

DISSENT: (Powell, J.) Sovereign immunity can only be waived in express and unequivocal terms. For immunity to have been waived here, something in the Act under which the lands were ceded would have to have indicated such a waiver.

▌ *ANALYSIS*

Prior to the present case, the Tucker Act had been narrowly construed. The general understanding was that the Act conferred jurisdiction but didn't constitute a waiver of immunity. The present action changed that.

FIDUCIARY DUTY A legal obligation to act for the benefit of another, including subordinating one's personal interests to that of the other person.

SOVEREIGN IMMUNITY Immunity of government from suit without its consent.

Quicknotes

TUCKER ACT Gives court of claims jurisdiction to render judgment against the government.

United States v. S.A. Empresa de Viacao Aerea Rio Grandense (Varig Airlines) et al.

Federal government (D) v. Airline (P)

467 U.S. 797 (1984).

NATURE OF CASE: Action for damages for negligent aircraft inspection.

FACT SUMMARY: Several lawsuits were filed against the Government (D) following airplane accidents allegedly due to mechanical or facility-related problems.

🏛 RULE OF LAW
Airplane certification is a discretionary governmental function not subject to tort liability.

FACTS: Two separate airplane accidents were allegedly due to substandard equipment, equipment which did not meet Federal Aviation Administration (FAA) regulations. The FAA had certified both airplanes. Following the accidents, numerous lawsuits were filed against numerous defendants, including the Government (D) for certifying substandard airplanes. The Government (D) contended that the policy was to "spot-check" airplanes to try to ensure compliance by manufacturers and that this policy was a discretionary governmental function exempt from the Tort Claims Act. The Ninth Circuit held, in all the actions, that the FAA actions were not exempt from the Act. All cases were consolidated for certiorari in the Supreme Court.

ISSUE: Is airplane certification a discretionary governmental function not subject to tort liability?

HOLDING AND DECISION: (Burger, C.J.) Yes. Airplane certification is a discretionary governmental function not subject to tort liability. The FAA is compelled, by statute, to adopt airplane safety regulations and to enforce compliance. The FAA came to the conclusion that the best use of scarce agency resources was to spot-check airplanes for violations rather than to exhaustively inspect each airplane. When an agency determines the extent to which it will supervise the safety procedures of private enterprise, it is performing a very basic discretionary function, precisely the type envisioned by the discretionary function exemption. The tort arena is not the proper forum for airing disagreements with regulatory policies, and this will not be permitted. Reversed.

▶ ANALYSIS

The Government (D) has at times argued for a very broad interpretation of the discretionary function exception. "Uniquely governmental" functions, it has been argued, should also be exempt. This position has never been adopted.

Quicknotes

49 U.S.C. § 1421 Directs Transportation Secretary to establish standards for aircraft designs.

FEDERAL TORTS CLAIMS ACT Allows civil actions against the United States.

FTCA, § 2680 Exempts discretionary functions from Act.

Gregoire v. Biddle

Immigrant (P) v. Governmental official (D)

177 F.2d 579 (2d Cir. 1949), 339 U.S. 949 (1950).

NATURE OF CASE: Suit for damages.

FACT SUMMARY: Gregoire (P) sued Biddle (D) and other government officials (D), alleging that they had maliciously caused him to be imprisoned on the knowingly false charge that he was an enemy alien.

🏛 RULE OF LAW
An agent of the government is immune from liability for the consequences of his actions, notwithstanding conduct actuated by malice.

FACTS: Gregoire (P) sued Biddle (D) and four other government officials (D), charging that they had caused him to be arrested and imprisoned as a German enemy alien although they knew he was actually French. Notwithstanding a ruling of the Enemy Alien Hearing Board, which had established that Gregoire (P) was a Frenchman, he was held in custody for almost five years before his release was ordered by a federal judge. Gregoire (P) alleged that his incarceration had been the result of the malicious and willful scheming of the officials (D) responsible for his arrest. The trial court acknowledged that the conduct of the officials (D) had been actuated solely by their ill will toward Gregoire (P) but dismissed the complaint on the ground that, by reason of their offices, the officials (D) enjoyed immunity from liability for the consequences of their acts.

ISSUE: Are government officials immune from liability for their malicious conduct toward private individuals?

HOLDING AND DECISION: (Hand, C.J.) Yes. Any agent of the government is immune from liability for the consequences of his acts, and this rule prevails even in cases in which the official's conduct was actuated by malice and personal spite. In *Yaselli v. Goff*, 275 U.S. 503 (1927), the malicious conduct of a government prosecutor was held to be protected by the same absolute privilege as applies to judges. Although ideally government officials should be called to account for actions which are motivated solely by personal ill will, it is necessary that the conduct of all officials be accorded immunity from liability if they are to be expected to carry out their duties. Unless these individuals could depend upon immunity from liability for the consequences of their acts, their unfettered performance of their duties would be curtailed and their effectiveness diminished as a result. Therefore, the rule according immunity to government officials operates to bar recovery by Gregoire (P) even if the actions of Biddle (D) and the others (D) were motivated by malice and spite. Affirmed.

▶ *ANALYSIS*

Originally, only judges enjoyed immunity from the consequences of their actions. Such cases as *Yaselli v. Goff* and *Gregoire v. Biddle* and subsequent cases eventually resulted in extension of the immunity doctrine to other officials as well. In fact, it is occasionally applied to private parties, provided the acts which they perform are carried out pursuant to governmental directives. Actions of state officials are generally also accorded immunity, although an exception to the immunity doctrine is recognized in cases involving Civil Rights Act violations.

Quicknotes

ABSOLUTE PRIVILEGE Complete immunity from liability for the communication of libelous or slanderous statements.

OFFICIAL IMMUNITY Immunity of an official from civil liability for injuries sustained by an individual as a result of actions performed in the discharge of his official duties.

QUALIFIED PRIVILEGE Immunity from liability for libelous or slanderous statements communicated in the execution of a political, judicial, social, or personal obligation, unless it is demonstrated that the statement was made with actual malice and knowledge of its falsity.

Barr v. Matteo

Housing agency official (D) v. Employee (P)

360 U.S. 564 (1959).

NATURE OF CASE: Appeal of award of damages for libel.

FACT SUMMARY: Two officials of an executive agency brought a libel action against the agency director for a press release criticizing them.

🏛 RULE OF LAW
Government officials are absolutely immune from defamation suits resulting from acts done in their official capacity.

FACTS: Barr (D), acting director of the Office of Housing Expediter, issued a press release, in response to comments made from the Senate floor, criticizing two of his subordinates and certain policies they endorsed. Matteo (P) and the other employee subsequently sued Barr (D) for libel. In the lower court, damages were awarded, and this was sustained on appeal.

ISSUE: Are government officials absolutely immune from defamation suits resulting from acts done in their official capacity?

HOLDING AND DECISION: (Harlan, J.) Yes. Governmental officials are absolutely immune from defamation suits resulting from acts done in their official capacity. It is important that government officials be free to exercise their duties free of the fear of the possibility of damage suits for their actions. Immunity has already been given to high government officials, but the same reasoning applies to lower officials as well. Generally speaking, the lower an official is, the narrower the protection will be, but it must be available all the same. Here, Barr (D) issued the press release to clarify his position on important issues and to respond to congressional criticism. This was an act within his official capacity, and he is entitled to immunity. Reversed.

CONCURRENCE: (Black, J.) Restrictions on official expression should come from Congress, not private libel suits.

DISSENT: (Warren, C.J.) The rule of the Court will serve to silence needed debate, for one criticizing an official will know that the official will be armed with immunity when the official counterattacks.

DISSENT: (Brennan, J.) Government officials should have qualified immunity, imposing liability only when malice could be shown.

▶ *ANALYSIS*

The plurality afforded government officials absolute immunity. The dissenters would have given them only a qualified immunity. The difference between the two is important. Under qualified immunity, a trial will likely occur; with absolute immunity, a trial is highly unlikely.

■■■

Quicknotes

IMMUNITY Exemption from a legal obligation.

MALICE The intention to commit an unlawful act with the intent to inflict injury without justification or excuse.

QUALIFIED IMMUNITY An affirmative defense relieving officials from civil liability for the performance of activities within their discretion so long as such conduct is not in violation of an individual's rights pursuant to law as determined by a reasonable person standard.

■■■

Bivens v. Six Unknown Named Agents of Federal Bureau of Narcotics

Private citizen (P) v. Law enforcement officers (D)

403 U.S. 388 (1971).

NATURE OF CASE: Appeal of dismissal of action for Fourth Amendment violations.

FACT SUMMARY: Six federal agents (D) conducted a warrantless search of Bivens' (P) apartment, resulting in his arrest.

 RULE OF LAW
A private cause of action for Fourth Amendment violations exists.

FACTS: Without a warrant, six federal agents (D) broke into Bivens's (P) apartment, conducted a search, and arrested him. Bivens (P) later brought an action for damages based upon Fourth Amendment violations. The district court dismissed, holding that the Amendment did not create a private right of action. The appellate court affirmed.

ISSUE: Does a private right of action for Fourth Amendment violations exist?

HOLDING AND DECISION: (Brennan, J.) Yes. A private right of action for Fourth Amendment violations exists. To hold otherwise would be to say the rights of private citizens against federal agents is the same as the rights of private citizens against other citizens. A federal agent, however, possesses a far greater capacity to do damage than does a private citizen. For this reason, a citizen's right of action against a federal agent should be broader than against other citizens. Also, the interests protected by state common law and the Fourth Amendment are not always coextensive, and a Fourth Amendment violation will not always be actionable under common law. For these reasons, a Fourth Amendment right of action should exist. Reversed.

CONCURRENCE: (Harlan, J.) Judicially created damage actions are permissible where such a remedy is necessary or appropriate and do not require a statutory basis.

DISSENT: (Burger, C.J.) The creation of a remedy such as the Court creates here is appropriate for Congress, not the courts, to authorize.

DISSENT: (Black, J.) The propriety of whether a remedy such as the Court fashions here is a matter for Congress, not the courts. The political issues involved deserve consideration in the political arena.

▌ ANALYSIS

There were two basic arguments against the creation of the remedy fashioned here. The first was that the specter of such suits would deter officials from vigorously executing their offices. The second was the argument advanced in the dissents.

■▬■

Quicknotes

FOURTH AMENDMENT Provides that persons be secure as to their person and private belongings against unreasonable searches and seizures.

■▬■

Butz v. Economou

Department of Agriculture (D) v. Commodities merchant (P)

438 U.S. 478 (1978).

NATURE OF CASE: Appeal of reversal of dismissal of action for damages against federal officials.

FACT SUMMARY: Economou (P) brought a damage action against various Department of Agriculture (D) officials who adjudicated a complaint against him.

🏛 RULE OF LAW
(1) Executive officials are entitled to qualified immunity for acts done outside the scope of their authority.
(2) Executive officials in an adjudicatory capacity are entitled to absolute immunity for acts done in their capacity.

FACTS: The Department of Agriculture (the Department) (D) filed a complaint against Economou (P) and his company, alleging that his company no longer had the financial requirements necessary for registration as a commodity futures merchant. The Hearing Examiner recommended sustaining the complaint. The Department (D) judicial officer affirmed. The Second Circuit, however, reversed. Economou (P) then filed an action for damages against the Department (D) and the hearing officers. The district court dismissed, holding that the individual defendants were absolutely immune. The Second Circuit reversed, holding that the officers were entitled only to a qualified immunity.

ISSUES:
(1) Are executive officials entitled to qualified immunity for acts done outside the scope of their authority?
(2) Are executive officials in an adjudicatory capacity entitled to absolute immunity for acts done in their capacity?

HOLDING AND DECISION: (White, J.)
(1) Yes. Executive officials are entitled to only a qualified immunity for acts done outside the scope of their authority.
(2) Yes. Adjudicatory officials are entitled to absolute immunity for acts done in their capacity. The clear rule throughout U.S. history is that both state and federal executive officials do not enjoy an absolute immunity for their official transgressions. Nothing in the law or logic compels the conclusion that federal officials may violate constitutional or statutory rights without fear of liability. It is sufficient to protect the public interest in freeing officials from fear of lawsuits to grant qualified immunity so that a plaintiff must prove malice. However, in this action, adjudicatory officials are involved. The law has long recognized the necessity that judicial officers, be completely free of the fear of damage lawsuits, and adjudicatory executive officials are no different in this respect. Therefore, absolute immunity is

extended to adjudicatory officials. Reversed as to the individual defendants.

CONCURRENCE AND DISSENT: (Rehnquist, J.)
The public interest in freeing officials to vigorously pursue their offices is sufficient to allow for the granting of absolute immunity.

▌ ANALYSIS

The Court had to find a way to distinguish *Barr v. Matteo*, 360 U.S. 564 (1959), which arguably was controlling here. First, *Barr* was only a plurality opinion. Second, in *Barr*, it was held that the defendant officer was still acting within the scope of his duties, something Economou (P) was claiming did not happen here.

■══■

Quicknotes

MALICE The intention to commit an unlawful act without justification or excuse.

QUALIFIED IMMUNITY An affirmative defense relieving officials from civil liability for the performance of activities within their discretion so long as such conduct is not in violation of an individual's rights pursuant to law as determined by a reasonable person standard.

■══■

CHAPTER 9

Beneficiary Enforcement of Public Law

Quick Reference Rules of Law

J.I. Case Co. v. Borak

Corporation (D) v. Shareholder (P)

377 U.S. 426 (1964).

NATURE OF CASE: Appeal of reversal of dismissal of shareholder's derivative action.

FACT SUMMARY: Borak (P) brought a shareholder's derivative action under § 14(a) of the Securities Exchange Act, for alleged misleading proxy statements.

🏛 RULE OF LAW
A private right of action for violations of § 14(a) of the Securities Exchange Act exists.

FACTS: Borak (P) brought a derivative action against J.I. Case Co. (D), claiming that a certain merger was brought about by misleading proxy statements in violation of § 14(a) of the 1934 Securities Exchange Act. The district court held that a private cause of action did not exist under § 14(a), except for declaratory relief. The district court dismissed. The court of appeals reversed, holding that such a right of action did exist. J.I. Case Co. (D) appealed.

ISSUE: Does a private right of action for violations of § 14(a) of the Securities Exchange Act, exist?

HOLDING AND DECISION: (Clark, J.) Yes. A private right of action for violations of § 14(a) of the Securities Exchange Act (the Act) exists. While no provision for a private right of action is made in the statute, it does not end the inquiry. The key question as to whether a private right of action is going to be implied is the extent to which implying such a right of action will further the legislative purposes of the Act. The Act states, that among its chief purposes is protection of investors, and a private right of action is certainly consistent with this purpose. Further, the type of injury that a § 14(a) violation will usually cause will be more directly felt by the corporation than by individual shareholders, so if a private right of action is to be implied, a derivative action should be implied also. Affirmed.

▶ ANALYSIS

The issue of implied rights of action is an old and persistent one. As legislation seldom spells out exactly what remedies will and will not be available, it is left to the courts to figure out exactly what Congress had in mind. The approach taken by the Court here was later refined in *Cort v. Ash*, 422 U.S. 66 (1975).

Cort v. Ash

Parties not identified.

422 U.S. 66 (1975).

NATURE OF CASE: Appeal of reversal of dismissal of action against corporate directors for violating federal rules against election contributions.

FACT SUMMARY: Ash (P) brought an action against certain corporate directors for contributing to the 1972 presidential election, contrary to federal law.

🏛 RULE OF LAW
A private right of action against corporate directors for authorizing corporate presidential election contributions does not exist.

FACTS: 18 U.S.C. § 610 made it a criminal offense for a corporation to contribute to presidential elections. Ash (P) brought an action against various corporate directors for alleged violations of this rule in the 1972 presidential election. Ash (P) sought both damages and injunctive relief. The district court dismissed, but the court of appeals reversed, holding that a private right of action existed. Cort (D) appealed.

ISSUE: Does a private right of action against corporate directors for authorizing corporate presidential election contributions exist?

HOLDING AND DECISION: (Brennan, J.) No. A private right of action against corporate directors for authorizing corporate presidential election contributions does not exist. The statute in question authorizes no such right of action, so one must be implied. With respect to injunctive relief, amendments to the statute specifically created an administrative mechanism for dealing with such violations starting with the 1976 election, so that would be the proper avenue for redress. With respect to implying a cause of action for damages, certain factors must be considered. First, was the plaintiff one of the class for whose benefit the statute was enacted? The answer is no, because the purpose of the statute was to keep presidential elections free from undue influence. Second, does anything in the legislative history suggest intent to imply a cause of action? The answer seems to be in the negative. Third, is such a right consistent with the purpose of the statute? Again, the purpose was to protect the integrity of elections, not corporate shareholders. Finally, is the area one traditionally left to state law? This would appear to be so, since corporations are created by the state and the state exercises primary control over them. For these reasons, a private right of action does not exist. Reversed.

▶ ANALYSIS

It is not clear from the language of the opinion whether the four factors discussed here were meant to be a final holding with respect to factors to be analyzed in future implied causes of action cases. To put it another way, will future cases discuss only these factors, or may others be introduced into the analysis? One would suspect the latter, but the Court did not say.

■■■■

Quicknotes

18 U.S.C. § 610 Prohibits corporate contributions to presidential candidates.

■■■■

Cannon v. University of Chicago

Medical student (P) v. College (D)

441 U.S. 677 (1979).

NATURE OF CASE: Appeal of dismissal of action for gender discrimination.

FACT SUMMARY: Cannon's (P) suit under Title IX of the Education Amendments of 1972 was dismissed, the court holding that a private right of action did not exist.

🏛 RULE OF LAW
A private right of action under Title IX to the Education Amendments of 1972 exists.

FACTS: Cannon (P) brought an action under Title IX of the Education Amendments of 1972 against the University of Chicago (D). The district court dismissed, holding that because the statute did not expressly create a private right of action, none existed. The court of appeals affirmed. Cannon (P) appealed.

ISSUE: Does a private right of action under Title IX of the Education Amendments of 1972 exist?

HOLDING AND DECISION: (Stevens, J.) Yes. A private right of action under Title IX of the Education Amendment of 1972 exists. Where a statute is silent as to whether a private right of action exists, a court must look to the four factors enunciated in *Cort v. Ash*, 422 U.S. 66 (1975), in deciding upon whether such a right of action is to be implied. First, the statute here was enacted for the class of persons of which Cannon (P) in this instance is a member, namely, women. Second, legislative history in this matter suggests that such a right is appropriate, as the statute is patterned after Title VI of the 1964 Civil Rights Act, to which a private right of action had been given prior to 1972. Third, a private right of action here would facilitate the underlying purpose of the statutory scheme. Finally, a federal remedy is appropriate here, as federal law has long been seen as the primary protector of individual rights. Reversed.

CONCURRENCE: (Rehnquist, J.) As Congress now knows the criteria used by the courts in deciding whether private rights of action exist, further creation of implied rights of action should be carefully scrutinized.

DISSENT: (White, J.) The statute here was directed toward federal agencies, not the institutions themselves.

DISSENT: (Powell, J.) Congress alone has power to confer jurisdiction upon lower federal courts; this Court was not given such authority. For that reason, implied rights of action are inappropriate.

▶ ANALYSIS

The jurisprudence of the Court with respect to implied private rights of action has been a mixed bag over the last decade. The Court, for instance, has not been enthusiastic about inferring such rights in business litigation, particularly in securities law and especially in Rule 10b-5 of the securities regulations. The Court has been more receptive to such rights of action in civil liberties cases.

Quicknotes

TITLE IX Prohibits sex discrimination by education programs receiving federal assistance.

TITLE VI Civil Rights Act created private remedy for violations.

Alexander v. Sandoval

State agency (D) v. Driver's license applicant (P)

532 U.S. 275 (2001).

NATURE OF CASE: Appeal from injunctive relief granted to private individuals suing to enforce disparate-impact regulations promulgated under Title VI of the Civil Rights Act of 1964.

FACT SUMMARY: When the Alabama Department of Public Safety (D) decided to administer driver's license examinations only in English, Sandoval (P), as representative of a class, sued the Alabama Department of Public Safety (D) to enjoin the examinations, arguing that the English-only examinations violated federal regulations promulgated under the anti-discriminatory provisions of the Civil Rights Act of 1964.

🏛 **RULE OF LAW**
Private individuals may not sue to enforce disparate-impact regulations promulgated under Title VI of the Civil Rights Act of 1964 in the absence of congressional intent.

FACTS: The Alabama Department of Public Safety (D) accepted grants of financial assistance from the United States Department of Justice (DOJ), thus subjecting itself to Title VI of the Civil Rights Act of 1964 (the Act), which precludes discrimination on the basis, among other things, of national origin. The Act authorizes federal agencies to effectuate provisions of the legislation by issuing rules, regulations, or orders of general applicability. The DOJ, accordingly, promulgated a regulation forbidding funding recipients from utilizing criteria or methods of administration having the effect of subjecting individuals to discrimination because of, among other things, their national origin. Alabama amended its Constitution in 1990 to declare English "the official language" of the state. Pursuant to this provision, the Alabama Department of Public Safety (D) decided to administer driver's license examinations only in English. Sandoval (P), as representative of a class, sued the Alabama Department of Public Safety (D) to enjoin English-only driver's examinations, arguing the English-only examinations violated the DOJ regulation. The federal district court agreed, and the court of appeals affirmed. The Alabama Department of Public Safety (D) appealed.

ISSUE: May private individuals sue to enforce disparate-impact regulations promulgated under Title VI of the Civil Rights Act of 1964 in the absence of Congressional intent?

HOLDING AND DECISION: (Scalia, J.) No. Private individuals may not sue to enforce disparate-impact regulations promulgated under Title VI of the Civil Rights Act of 1964 (the Act) in the absence of Congressional intent. The argument of Sandoval (P) that the regulations contain rights-creating language and so must be privately enforceable, skips an analytical step. Language in a regulation may invoke a private right of action that Congress through statutory text created, but it may not create a right that Congress has not. Thus, when, as here, a statute has provided a general authorization for private enforcement of regulations, it may perhaps be correct that the intent displayed in each regulation can determine whether or not it is privately enforceable. However, it is most certainly incorrect to say that language can conjure up a private cause of action that has not been authorized by Congress. Agencies may play the sorcerer's apprentice but not the sorcerer himself. Statutes, such as here, that focus on the person regulated rather than the individuals protected create "no implication of intent to confer rights on a particular class of persons." Nor do the methods that the Act goes on to provide for enforcing its authorized regulations manifest an intent to create a private remedy; if anything, they suggest the opposite. Reversed.

DISSENT: (Stevens, J.) There is a clear precedent of the Supreme Court for the proposition that injunctive relief is proper in a case of this type through an "implied right of action." Here, the "legislative design" reflects a reasonable—indeed inspired—model for attacking the often-intractable problem of racial and ethnic discrimination.

▶ *ANALYSIS*

In the *Alexander* decision, the Supreme Court notes that the express provision of one method of enforcing a substantive rule suggests that Congress intended to preclude others. Far from displaying Congressional intent to create new rights, the Act limits agencies to "effectuating" rights already created by the statute.

■=■

Quicknotes

PRIVATE RIGHT OF ACTION A fact or set of facts, the occurrence of which entitle a party to seek judicial relief.

■=■

Maine v. Thiboutot

State government (D) v. Welfare recipient (P)

448 U.S. 1 (1980).

NATURE OF CASE: Appeal of award of damages in action for welfare benefits.

FACT SUMMARY: Thiboutot (P) brought suit under 42 U.S.C. § 1983 to recover welfare benefits alleged to be wrongfully withheld.

🏛 RULE OF LAW
42 U.S.C. § 1983 encompasses claims brought on purely statutory grounds.

FACTS: The State of Maine (D) determined that Thiboutot (P) was no longer entitled to certain welfare benefits he had been receiving under 42 U.S.C. § 602(a)(7). Thiboutot (P) brought an action to recover the benefits under both state law and 42 U.S.C. § 1983. The trial court granted relief under § 1983. The state supreme court upheld this and awarded attorney fees under 42 U.S.C. § 1988, as well. Maine (D) appealed.

ISSUE: Does 42 U.S.C. § 1983 encompass claims brought on purely statutory grounds?

HOLDING AND DECISION: (Brennan, J.) Yes. 42 U.S.C. § 1983 encompasses claims brought on purely statutory grounds. The wording of § 1983 permits actions based not only on constitutional violations but on violations of "laws" as well. Nothing in the legislative history shows that the meaning of "laws" in the context of the statute should be anything other than the plain meaning of the word. Finally, dicta in numerous prior opinions of this Court have opined that § 1983 included statutory as well as constitutional violations. Affirmed.

DISSENT: (Powell, J.) The legislative history clearly shows that § 1983 was meant to apply only in civil rights actions, not in all actions based on federal statutory violations.

▶ ANALYSIS

Justice Powell rather disconcertedly called this a landmark opinion, and although it is too early to tell, it certainly could prove to be such. Section 1983 has for several decades been the primary vehicle for private enforcement of civil rights. The ability of a successful plaintiff to recover attorney fees makes it all the more attractive. This will be a powerful tool in lawsuits against government officials.

■═■

Quicknotes

42 U.S.C. § 1983 Provides a cause of action against persons who violate rights under color of law.

42 U.S.C. § 1988 Allows for attorney fees to be awarded the prevailing party in an action pursuant to § 1983.

■═■

Pennhurst State School and Hospital v. Halderman

Facility for persons with disabilities (D) v. Unidentified citizen (P)

451 U.S. 1 (1981).

NATURE OF CASE: Appeal of order compelling compliance with federal mental health care standards.

FACT SUMMARY: Halderman (P) and others brought an action against Pennhurst State School and Hospital (D) to compel compliance with federal laws regarding minimum adequate care of people with mental disabilities.

🏛 RULE OF LAW
The Developmentally Disabled Assistance and Bill of Rights Act, does not obligate the states to provide a certain level of care to people with mental disabilities.

FACTS: The Developmentally Disabled Assistance and Bill of Rights Act of 1975 (the Act) established a voluntary program wherein states could receive federal funds in exchange for instituting certain programs to aid people with mental disabilities. A portion of the Act was codified at 42 U.S.C. § 6010 and established that people with mental disabilities had certain "rights" with respect to minimum levels of care. The section contained no language to the effect that meeting the standards was necessary for a state to receive funds. Halderman (P) and others brought an action against Pennhurst State School and Hospital (D), a state institution, to enforce compliance with the standards articulated in § 6010. The district court ordered compliance with the standards, and the court of appeals affirmed.

ISSUE: Does the Developmentally Disabled Assistance and Bill of Rights Act obligate the states to provide a certain level of care to people with mental disabilities?

HOLDING AND DECISION: (Rehnquist, J.) No. The Developmentally Disabled Assistance and Bill of Rights Act (the Act) does not obligate the states to provide a certain level of care to people with mental disabilities. The Act is a voluntary one and imposes no affirmative duties upon the states beyond the extent necessary per the terms of the Act for the states to receive funds. Importantly, the terms of § 6010, unlike other sections, do not make compliance a condition for receiving funds. This Court is unwilling to read conditions into a voluntary program, for such programs are akin to contracts, and courts should not read terms into contracts which are unambiguous. Since compliance with § 6010 is not textually a condition for receipt of payments, this Court will not hold that it is. Reversed.

DISSENT: (White, J.) The standards articulated in § 6010 are integral to the Act, and compliance should be a necessary condition of participation. The case should have been remanded to the lower courts for the fashioning of an appropriate remedy.

▶ ANALYSIS

The plaintiffs asserted that compliance with the standards was mandated by two distinct sources of congressional power. The first was the spending power. The second was the appropriate legislation section of the Fourteenth Amendment. The Court completely rejected the latter as a possible reason for compliance, as it arguably would have imposed its standards on the states regardless of whether the state had elected to participate in the program.

■══■

Quicknotes

42 U.S.C. § 6000 Developmentally Disabled Assistance and Bill of Rights Act.

42 U.S.C. § 6010 Bill of Rights provision giving disabled the right to appropriate treatment and services.

■══■

Gonzaga University v. John Doe

Private university (D) v. Student (P)

536 U.S. 273 (2002).

NATURE OF CASE: Appeal from a decision permitting a private suit under a federal statute.

FACT SUMMARY: John Doe (Doe) (P), a former Gonzaga University (Gonzaga) (D) student, sued Gonzaga (D) for damages under 42 U.S.C. § 1983 when he was denied a state teaching position because of personal information supplied to the state from Doe's (P) personnel file at Gonzaga (D) in violation of the Family Educational Rights and Privacy Act of 1974.

> **RULE OF LAW**
> 42 U.S.C. § 1983 does not permit a student to sue a private university for damages to enforce the Family Educational Rights and Privacy Act of 1974.

FACTS: John Doe (Doe) (P), a former undergraduate at private Gonzaga University (Gonzaga) (D), planned to teach at a Washington elementary school. Washington required affidavits of good moral character. Gonzaga (D) turned over to Washington damaging information contained in Doe's (P) Gonzaga personnel file, which prevented Doe (P) from obtaining the teaching position for which he had applied. Doe (P) brought a private damages suit against Gonzaga (D), alleging that 42 U.S.C. § 1983 permitted a student to sue a private university for damages to enforce the Family Educational Rights and Privacy Act of 1974 (FERPA). Doe's (P) argument was that FERPA prohibits the federal funding of educational institutions that have a policy or practice of releasing educational records to unauthorized persons. The state trial court agreed and awarded damages to Doe (P). The state appellate court reversed; however, the state's supreme court reversed the appellate court and reinstated Doe's (P) award. Gonzaga (D) appealed to the U.S. Supreme Court.

ISSUE: Does 42 U.S.C. § 1983 permit a student to sue a private university for damages to enforce the Family Educational Rights and Privacy Act of 1974?

HOLDING AND DECISION: (Rehnquist, C.J.) No. 42 U.S.C. § 1983 does not permit a student to sue a private university for damages to enforce the Family Educational Rights and Privacy Act of 1974. FERPA's nondisclosure provisions speak only in terms of institutional policy and practice, not individual instances of disclosure. Hence, the statutory provisions have an "aggregate" focus and are not concerned with whether the needs of any particular person have been satisfied. Recipient institutions can further avoid termination of funding as long as they comply substantially with the act's requirements. Section 1983 provides a remedy only for the deprivation of rights, privileges, or immunities secured by the Constitution and laws of the United States.

Accordingly, it is "rights," not the broader or vaguer "benefits" or "interests" that may be enforced under the authority of the statute. The question whether Congress intended to create a private right of action is, as here, definitely answered in the negative where the statute by its terms grants no private rights to any identifiable class. For a statute to create such private rights, the text must be phrased in terms of the persons benefited. FERPA's provisions "speak only to the Secretary of Education." Reversed.

CONCURRENCE: (Breyer, J.) The Court should not, in effect, predetermine an outcome through the use of a presumption such as the majority's presumption that a right is conferred only if set forth "unambiguously" in a statute's "text and structure." While factors set forth in the Court's § 1983 cases are helpful indications of congressional intent, the statute books are too many, the laws too diverse, and their purposes too complex, for any single legal formula to offer more than general guidance.

DISSENT: (Stevens, J.) The FERPA in its entirety creates rights for both students and their parents and describes the procedures for enforcing and protecting those rights. The statutory provisions, while not as explicit as in some other legislation, plainly meet the standards articulated by the Court for establishing a federal right to individuals for enforcement: It is directed to the benefit of individual students and parents; the provision is binding on states; and the right is far from vague and amorphous.

ANALYSIS

The Court in *Gonzaga* observed that its conclusion that FERPA failed to confer enforceable rights to private individuals was buttressed by the various mechanisms that Congress chose to provide for enforcing the statute's provisions.

Quicknotes

PRIVATE RIGHT OF ACTION A fact or set of facts, the occurrence of which entitle a party to seek judicial relief.

Nader v. Allegheny Airlines, Inc.

Airline passenger (P) v. Airline (D)

426 U.S. 290 (1976).

NATURE OF CASE: Appeal of issuance of stay of judgment in action for damages pending review by the Civil Aeronautics Board.

FACT SUMMARY: Nader (P), "bumped" from an airline flight due to overbooking, brought an action against Allegheny Airlines, Inc. (D), claiming the practice to be deceptive.

🏛 RULE OF LAW
A common-law fraud action against an airline is not dependent on § 411 of the Federal Aviation Act of 1958.

FACTS: Nader (P) made a reservation on a flight with Allegheny Airlines, Inc. (Allegheny) (D). Nader (P) was "bumped" due to Allegheny's (D) practice of overbooking. Nader (P) and the Connecticut Citizen Action Group (P), whose meeting he had missed as a result of being denied his reserved plane seat, brought an action against Allegheny (D), contending that overbooking constituted fraudulent misrepresentation. A district court awarded $61 in compensatory damages and $50,000 in punitive damages. The appellate court issued a stay. It held that since § 411 of the Federal Aviation Act of 1958 gave the Civil Aeronautics Board (CAB) the power to force an airline to cease deceptive practices, a determination by the CAB that a practice was not deceptive would preclude a common-law tort action. The court held that the CAB must first determine whether the practice was deceptive.

ISSUE: Is a common-law fraud action against an airline dependent on § 411 of the Federal Aviation Act of 1958?

HOLDING AND DECISION: (Powell, J.) No. A common-law fraud action against an airline is not dependent on § 411 of the Federal Aviation Act of 1958. Section 411 is not available to consumers but only to the CAB. Also, the scope of § 411 is not coextensive with common-law fraud because the CAB acting under § 411 need not find intention or actual damages to implement a cease-and-desist order. Since § 411 differs in its reach from common fraud, this Court sees it as a supplement to common-law fraud but not a replacement. Reversed.

CONCURRENCE: (White, J.) It is doubtful that a decision by the CAB here would add anything to what it has already concluded regarding overbooking.

▶ *ANALYSIS*

Statutes sometimes are held to preempt traditional common-law rights of action. However, courts generally do not like to hold this. More likely, a court will hold, as the Court did here, that the remedies are nonexclusive. Sometimes the administrative procedure will be held to be the first resort, with court action available only after the administrative procedures have been concluded.

■══■

Quicknotes

FEDERAL AVIATION ACT, § 411 Allows the Federal Aviation Administration to investigate and determine whether airlines are engaged in deceptive practices.

■══■

Alexis Geier v. American Honda Motor Company, Inc.

Driver (P) v. Car manufacturer (D)

529 U.S. 861 (2000).

NATURE OF CASE: Appeal from a dismissal of state tort suit.

FACT SUMMARY: In reviewing dismissal, the court of appeals found that Alexis Geier's state tort claim conflicted with the purposes of the National Traffic and Motor Vehicle Safety Act of 1966 and was therefore preempted.

RULE OF LAW

A common-law claim that actually conflicts with a federal statute's purposes is preempted by the same statute.

FACTS: Under the authority of the National Traffic and Motor Vehicle Safety Act of 1966 (the Safety Act), the Department of Transportation promulgated a safety standard (FMVSS 208) requiring auto manufacturers to equip some, but not all of their 1987 vehicles with passive restraints. Alexis Geier (Geier) (P) was seriously injured when the 1987 Honda Accord she was driving collided with a tree. Geier (P) sued American Honda Motor Co., Inc. (D) under D.C. tort law for failure to equip the car with a driver-side airbag. The district court dismissed the suit on the grounds of express preemption by the safety statute. The court of appeals affirmed the dismissal, but on the ground of conflict preemption rather than express preemption.

ISSUE: Does a common-law "no-airbag" action actually conflict with FMVSS 208?

HOLDING AND DECISION: (Breyer, J.) Yes. According to the Department of Transportation (DOT) comments that accompanied FMVSS 208, the standard deliberately provided car manufacturers with a range of choices among different passive restraints to gradually introduce a mix of different devices, lower costs, encourage technological development and win widespread consumer acceptance. Further, DOT rejected an all airbag standard because of safety concerns associated with airbags. Finally, FMVSS 208's passive restraint requirement was conditional, providing for rescission of its passive restraint requirement if, by September 1, 1989, two-thirds of the States had laws in place that required auto occupants to buckle up. Imposing a state law duty to impose airbags in all vehicles would present an obstacle to the goals of FMVSS 208.

DISSENT: (Stevens, J.) Under ordinary experience-proven principles of conflict preemption, the presumption against preemption should control. Instead, here the Court wrongly simply ignores the presumption, preferring instead to put the burden on Geier (P) to show that its tort claim would not frustrate the federal statute's purposes. Even in cases where implied regulatory preemption is at issue, the

Court generally expects an administrative regulation to declare any intention to preempt state law with some specificity. Here, this was not done. Neither Standard 208 nor its accompanying commentary includes the slightest specific intention to preempt common-law no-airbag suits. Indeed, the only mention of such suits in the commentary tends to suggest that they would not be preempted. There is no showing that allowing this common-law suit would impose an obligation on vehicle manufacturers which would directly and irreconcilably contradict the primary objectives of Standard 208.

ANALYSIS

The Safety Act in *Geier* contained an express preemption provision, but it also contained a savings clause which removed tort actions such as Geier's (P) from the scope of the express preemption clause. Congress more commonly uses language indicating a desire to preempt state law only partially. Many "partial preemption" statutes delegate to federal regulatory agencies the power to sanction the potentially conflicting exercise of state jurisdiction.

■=■

Quicknotes

PREEMPTION Judicial preference recognizing, the procedure of federal legislation over state legislation of the same subject matter.

■=■

Bates v. Dow Agrosciences LLC

Farmers (P) v. Pesticide manufacturer (D)

544 U.S. 431 (2005).

NATURE OF CASE: Petition for declaratory judgment.

FACT SUMMARY: Twenty-nine Texas peanut farmers (P) claimed that in the 2000 growing season their crops were damaged after application of Dow Agrosciences (D) new pesticide named "Strongarm."

🏛 RULE OF LAW
The Federal Insecticide, Fungicide, and Rodenticide Act does not preempt farmers' state tort claims alleging that a pesticide manufacturer damaged crops.

FACTS: A group of peanut farmers (P) in Texas threatened to sue Dow Agrosciences (D) in state court for damages caused by one of Dow's (D) pesticides. The farmers (P) alleged Dow (D) violated Texas labeling requirements because its label failed to warn against use on high-pH soil. Dow (D) had complied with federal regulatory requirements, and therefore asked a federal district court to rule the Federal Insecticide, Fungicide and Rodenticide Act (FIFRA) preempted and prohibited the farmers' (P) state law claims. The district court and the U.S. Court of Appeals for the Fifth Circuit ruled FIFRA expressly prohibited additional state labeling requirements such as that by Texas.

ISSUE: Does the Federal Insecticide, Fungicide, and Rodenticide Act preempt farmers' state tort claims alleging that a pesticide manufacturer damaged crops?

HOLDING AND DECISION: (Stevens, J.) No. The Federal Insecticide, Fungicide, and Rodenticide Act (FIFRA), does not preempt farmers' state tort claims alleging that a pesticide manufacturer damaged crops. FIFRA preempts only state-law requirements for labeling or packaging. The peanut farmers' (P) defective manufacture, negligent testing, and breach of warranty claims were based on common law and did not necessarily require that Dow (D) label products in a specific way. The farmers' (P) fraud and negligent-failure to warn claims were based on common law rules that qualified as requirements for labeling or packaging. But because FIFRA preempted only state-law labeling requirements that were "in addition to or different from" FIFRA's labeling standards, the peanut farmers (P) can sue Dow (D) in state court.

CONCURRENCE: (Breyer, J.) State law requirements must be measured against the relevant Environmental Protection Agency regulations that give content to FIFRA's misbranding standards.

DISSENT: (Thomas, J.) A state-law cause of action by the farmers (P), even if not specific to labeling, still imposes a labeling requirement in addition to, or different from, FIFRA's when it attaches liability to statements on the label that do not produce liability under FIFRA. Therefore, state-law causes of action should be remanded for preemption analysis.

▶ ANALYSIS

It is important to note that under the decision in this case, buyers of pesticides and herbicides can bring state law tort claims against the product manufacturer even where the product and the product label comply with all federal regulatory requirements.

■━■

Quicknotes

PREEMPTION Doctrine holding that matters of national interest take precedence over matters of local interest; the federal law takes precedence over state law.

■━■

Wyeth v. Levine

Drug manufacturer (D) v. Patient (P)

555 U.S. ___, 129 S. Ct. 1187 (2009).

NATURE OF CASE: Appeal of state supreme court decision.

FACT SUMMARY: After complications resulting from the injection of a drug into her arm resulted in amputation, [Diana] Levine (P) filed a personal injury action against Wyeth (D), the drug manufacturer.

🏛 RULE OF LAW
Federal law does not preempt state law in a personal injury action against a drug manufacturer for failing to include an appropriate warning label where the drug in question met federal labeling requirements.

FACTS: [Diana] Levine (P) had Phenergan, a drug made by Wyeth (D) and intended to prevent allergies and motion sickness, injected into her arm. Complications from the injection led to the amputation of her arm. Levine (P) argued that Wyeth (D) failed to include a warning label describing the possible arterial injuries that could occur from negligent injection of the drug. Wyeth (D) argued that because their warning label had been deemed acceptable by the Food and Drug Administration (FDA), a federal agency, any Vermont state regulations making the label insufficient were preempted. The Superior Court of Vermont found in favor of Levine (P) and denied Wyeth's (D) motion for a new trial. The Supreme Court of Vermont affirmed, holding that the FDA requirements merely provide a floor, not a ceiling, for state regulation. Therefore, states are free to create more stringent labeling requirements than federal law provides.

ISSUE: Does federal law preempt state law in a personal injury action against a drug manufacturer for failing to include an appropriate warning label where the drug in question met federal labeling requirements?

HOLDING AND DECISION: (Stevens, J.) No. Federal law does not preempt state law in a personal injury action against a drug manufacturer for failing to include an appropriate warning label where the drug in question met federal labeling requirements. Wyeth's (D) argument that by unilaterally changing its labeling of Phenergan, it would have violated federal labeling regulations is rejected. The manufacturer bears ultimate responsibility for the content of its labels at all times. Wyeth's (D) argument that requiring it to comply with the state-law duty to provide a stronger warning would interfere with Congress' purpose of entrusting the FDA with drug labeling decisions is also rejected. Congress did not intend to preempt state-law failure to warn actions when it created the Food, Drug, and Cosmetic Act.

CONCURRENCE: (Breyer, J.) The FDA may create regulations that preempt state law tort claims, but such a regulation was not at issue in this case.

CONCURRENCE: (Thomas, J.) The majority opinion implicitly endorses a "far-reaching implied preemption doctrine" under which the court invalidates state laws based on perceived conflicts with federal statutes by extrapolating from evidence not found in the text of the statute itself.

DISSENT: (Alito, J.) The court's holding that a jury, rather than the FDA, is ultimately responsible for regulating warning labels for prescription drugs is wrong because it is incompatible with court precedent on the issue of preemption.

▶ ANALYSIS

This decision allows lawsuits in state courts to compensate for missteps at the national level. Six of the justices joined in upholding the verdict in favor of Levine (P) of nearly $6.8 million against Wyeth (D), and the decision no doubt sent a powerful message to the pharmaceutical industry, as well as federal agencies. Under the decision, drug companies are primarily responsible for keeping their warning labels up to date and complete, and the FDA not only needs to police the industry more closely, despite limited resources, but also may not silence patients' grievances brought through state courts without crystal-clear support from Congress.

■▬■

Quicknotes

FOOD AND DRUG ADMINISTRATION A federal agency responsible for establishing safety and quality standards for foods, drugs, and cosmetics.

■▬■

Glossary

Common Latin Words and Phrases Encountered in the Law

A FORTIORI: Because one fact exists or has been proven, therefore a second fact that is related to the first fact must also exist.

A PRIORI: From the cause to the effect. A term of logic used to denote that when one generally accepted truth is shown to be a cause, another particular effect must necessarily follow.

AB INITIO: From the beginning; a condition which has existed throughout, as in a marriage which was void ab initio.

ACTUS REUS: The wrongful act; in criminal law, such action sufficient to trigger criminal liability.

AD VALOREM: According to value; an ad valorem tax is imposed upon an item located within the taxing jurisdiction calculated by the value of such item.

AMICUS CURIAE: Friend of the court. Its most common usage takes the form of an amicus curiae brief, filed by a person who is not a party to an action but is nonetheless allowed to offer an argument supporting his legal interests.

ARGUENDO: In arguing. A statement, possibly hypothetical, made for the purpose of argument, is one made arguendo.

BILL QUIA TIMET: A bill to quiet title (establish ownership) to real property.

BONA FIDE: True, honest, or genuine. May refer to a person's legal position based on good faith or lacking notice of fraud (such as a bona fide purchaser for value) or to the authenticity of a particular document (such as a bona fide last will and testament).

CAUSA MORTIS: With approaching death in mind. A gift causa mortis is a gift given by a party who feels certain that death is imminent.

CAVEAT EMPTOR: Let the buyer beware. This maxim is reflected in the rule of law that a buyer purchases at his own risk because it is his responsibility to examine, judge, test, and otherwise inspect what he is buying.

CERTIORARI: A writ of review. Petitions for review of a case by the United States Supreme Court are most often done by means of a writ of certiorari.

CONTRA: On the other hand. Opposite. Contrary to.

CORAM NOBIS: Before us; writs of error directed to the court that originally rendered the judgment.

CORAM VOBIS: Before you; writs of error directed by an appellate court to a lower court to correct a factual error.

CORPUS DELICTI: The body of the crime; the requisite elements of a crime amounting to objective proof that a crime has been committed.

CUM TESTAMENTO ANNEXO, ADMINISTRATOR (ADMINISTRATOR C.T.A.): With will annexed; an administrator c.t.a. settles an estate pursuant to a will in which he is not appointed.

DE BONIS NON, ADMINISTRATOR (ADMINISTRATOR D.B.N.): Of goods not administered; an administrator d.b.n. settles a partially settled estate.

DE FACTO: In fact; in reality; actually. Existing in fact but not officially approved or engendered.

DE JURE: By right; lawful. Describes a condition that is legitimate "as a matter of law," in contrast to the term "de facto," which connotes something existing in fact but not legally sanctioned or authorized. For example, de facto segregation refers to segregation brought about by housing patterns, etc., whereas de jure segregation refers to segregation created by law.

DE MINIMIS: Of minimal importance; insignificant; a trifle; not worth bothering about.

DE NOVO: Anew; a second time; afresh. A trial de novo is a new trial held at the appellate level as if the case originated there and the trial at a lower level had not taken place.

DICTA: Generally used as an abbreviated form of obiter dicta, a term describing those portions of a judicial opinion incidental or not necessary to resolution of the specific question before the court. Such nonessential statements and remarks are not considered to be binding precedent.

DUCES TECUM: Refers to a particular type of writ or subpoena requesting a party or organization to produce certain documents in their possession.

EN BANC: Full bench. Where a court sits with all justices present rather than the usual quorum.

EX PARTE: For one side or one party only. An ex parte proceeding is one undertaken for the benefit of only one party, without notice to, or an appearance by, an adverse party.

EX POST FACTO: After the fact. An ex post facto law is a law that retroactively changes the consequences of a prior act.

EX REL.: Abbreviated form of the term "ex relatione," meaning upon relation or information. When the state brings an action in which it has no interest against an individual at the instigation of one who has a private interest in the matter.

FORUM NON CONVENIENS: Inconvenient forum. Although a court may have jurisdiction over the case, the action should be tried in a more conveniently located court, one to which parties and witnesses may more easily travel, for example.

GUARDIAN AD LITEM: A guardian of an infant as to litigation, appointed to represent the infant and pursue his/her rights.

HABEAS CORPUS: You have the body. The modern writ of habeas corpus is a writ directing that a person (body) being detained (such as a prisoner) be brought before the court so that the legality of his detention can be judicially ascertained.

IN CAMERA: In private, in chambers. When a hearing is held before a judge in his chambers or when all spectators are excluded from the courtroom.

IN FORMA PAUPERIS: In the manner of a pauper. A party who proceeds in forma pauperis because of his poverty is one who is allowed to bring suit without liability for costs.

INFRA: Below, under. A word referring the reader to a later part of a book. (The opposite of supra.)

IN LOCO PARENTIS: In the place of a parent.

IN PARI DELICTO: Equally wrong; a court of equity will not grant requested relief to an applicant who is in pari delicto, or as much at fault in the transactions giving rise to the controversy as is the opponent of the applicant.

IN PARI MATERIA: On like subject matter or upon the same matter. Statutes relating to the same person or things are said to be in pari materia. It is a general rule of statutory construction that such statutes should be construed together, i.e., looked at as if they together constituted one law.

IN PERSONAM: Against the person. Jurisdiction over the person of an individual.

IN RE: In the matter of. Used to designate a proceeding involving an estate or other property.

IN REM: A term that signifies an action against the res, or thing. An action in rem is basically one that is taken directly against property, as distinguished from an action in personam, i.e., against the person.

INTER ALIA: Among other things. Used to show that the whole of a statement, pleading, list, statute, etc., has not been set forth in its entirety.

INTER PARTES: Between the parties. May refer to contracts, conveyances or other transactions having legal significance.

INTER VIVOS: Between the living. An inter vivos gift is a gift made by a living grantor, as distinguished from bequests contained in a will, which pass upon the death of the testator.

IPSO FACTO: By the mere fact itself.

JUS: Law or the entire body of law.

LEX LOCI: The law of the place; the notion that the rights of parties to a legal proceeding are governed by the law of the place where those rights arose.

MALUM IN SE: Evil or wrong in and of itself; inherently wrong. This term describes an act that is wrong by its very nature, as opposed to one which would not be wrong but for the fact that there is a specific legal prohibition against it (malum prohibitum).

MALUM PROHIBITUM: Wrong because prohibited, but not inherently evil. Used to describe something that is wrong because it is expressly forbidden by law but that is not in and of itself evil, e.g., speeding.

MANDAMUS: We command. A writ directing an official to take a certain action.

MENS REA: A guilty mind; a criminal intent. A term used to signify the mental state that accompanies a crime or other prohibited act. Some crimes require only a general mens rea (general intent to do the prohibited act), but others, like assault with intent to murder, require the existence of a specific mens rea.

MODUS OPERANDI: Method of operating; generally refers to the manner or style of a criminal in committing crimes, admissible in appropriate cases as evidence of the identity of a defendant.

NEXUS: A connection to.

NISI PRIUS: A court of first impression. A nisi prius court is one where issues of fact are tried before a judge or jury.

N.O.V. (NON OBSTANTE VEREDICTO): Notwithstanding the verdict. A judgment n.o.v. is a judgment given in favor of one party despite the fact that a verdict was returned in favor of the other party, the justification being that the verdict either had no reasonable support in fact or was contrary to law.

NUNC PRO TUNC: Now for then. This phrase refers to actions that may be taken and will then have full retroactive effect.

PENDENTE LITE: Pending the suit; pending litigation under way.

PER CAPITA: By head; beneficiaries of an estate, if they take in equal shares, take per capita.

PER CURIAM: By the court; signifies an opinion ostensibly written "by the whole court" and with no identified author.

PER SE: By itself, in itself; inherently.

PER STIRPES: By representation. Used primarily in the law of wills to describe the method of distribution where a person, generally because of death, is unable to take that which is left to him by the will of another, and therefore his heirs divide such property between them rather than take under the will individually.

PRIMA FACIE: On its face, at first sight. A prima facie case is one that is sufficient on its face, meaning that the evidence supporting it is adequate to establish the case until contradicted or overcome by other evidence.

PRO TANTO: For so much; as far as it goes. Often used in eminent domain cases when a property owner receives partial payment for his land without prejudice to his right to bring suit for the full amount he claims his land to be worth.

QUANTUM MERUIT: As much as he deserves. Refers to recovery based on the doctrine of unjust enrichment in those cases in which a party has rendered valuable services or furnished materials that were accepted and enjoyed by another under circumstances that would reasonably notify the recipient that the rendering party expected to be paid. In essence, the law implies a contract to pay the reasonable value of the services or materials furnished.

QUASI: Almost like; as if; nearly. This term is essentially used to signify that one subject or thing is almost analogous to another but that material differences between them do exist. For example, a quasi-criminal proceeding is one that is not strictly criminal but shares enough of the same characteristics to require some of the same safeguards (e.g., procedural due process must be followed in a parole hearing).

QUID PRO QUO: Something for something. In contract law, the consideration, something of value, passed between the parties to render the contract binding.

RES GESTAE: Things done; in evidence law, this principle justifies the admission of a statement that would otherwise be hearsay when it is made so closely to the event in question as to be said to be a part of it, or with such spontaneity as not to have the possibility of falsehood.

RES IPSA LOQUITUR: The thing speaks for itself. This doctrine gives rise to a rebuttable presumption of negligence when the instrumentality causing the injury was within the exclusive control of the defendant, and the injury was one that does not normally occur unless a person has been negligent.

RES JUDICATA: A matter adjudged. Doctrine which provides that once a court of competent jurisdiction has rendered a final judgment or decree on the merits, that judgment or decree is conclusive upon the parties to the case and prevents them from engaging in any other litigation on the points and issues determined therein.

RESPONDEAT SUPERIOR: Let the master reply. This doctrine holds the master liable for the wrongful acts of his servant (or the principal for his agent) in those cases in which the servant (or agent) was acting within the scope of his authority at the time of the injury.

STARE DECISIS: To stand by or adhere to that which has been decided. The common law doctrine of stare decisis attempts to give security and certainty to the law by following the policy that once a principle of law as applicable to a certain set of facts has been set forth in a decision, it forms a precedent which will subsequently be followed, even though a different decision might be made were it the first time the question had arisen. Of course, stare decisis is not an inviolable principle and is departed from in instances where there is good cause (e.g., considerations of public policy led the Supreme Court to disregard prior decisions sanctioning segregation).

SUPRA: Above. A word referring a reader to an earlier part of a book.

ULTRA VIRES: Beyond the power. This phrase is most commonly used to refer to actions taken by a corporation that are beyond the power or legal authority of the corporation.

Addendum of French Derivatives

IN PAIS: Not pursuant to legal proceedings.

CHATTEL: Tangible personal property.

CY PRES: Doctrine permitting courts to apply trust funds to purposes not expressed in the trust but necessary to carry out the settlor's intent.

PER AUTRE VIE: For another's life; during another's life. In property law, an estate may be granted that will terminate upon the death of someone other than the grantee.

PROFIT A PRENDRE: A license to remove minerals or other produce from land.

VOIR DIRE: Process of questioning jurors as to their predispositions about the case or parties to a proceeding in order to identify those jurors displaying bias or prejudice.

Casenote Legal Briefs